TEACHINGS

OF

ISLAM

Members of the *Aḥmadiyyah Anjuman Ishā'at Islām* (Lahore - West Pakistan) believe that:

— After the holy Prophet Muḥammad (Peace be upon him), God has barred the appearance of any prophet, new or old.

— Angel Gabriel cannot bring 'prophetic revelation' to any person as this would contradict the two complementary verses: "This day have I perfected for you your religion" (5 : 3); "Muḥammad is the Messenger of Allāh and the Seal of the prophets" (33 : 40). It would otherwise violate the sanctity of finality of prophethood in Islam.

— All the Companions of the Holy Prophet Muḥammad (*aṣḥāb*) and all the spiritual leaders (*imām*) are venerable.

— It is incumbent to believe in the missions of all reformers (*mujaddid*).

— He who believes that "there is no God but Allāh and Muḥammad is His Prophet" (*kalimah*) cannot be regarded an unbeliever or infidel (*kāfir*).

— No verse of the holy Quran has been, or shall ever be, abrogated.

HAZRAT MIRZA GHULAM AHMAD
Mujaddid (Reformer) of the 14th Century Hijrah

TEACHINGS OF ISLAM

Translation :

MAULANA MUHAMMAD ALI

AHMADIYYA ANJUMAN ISHA'AT ISLAM LAHORE U.S.A.
1315 Kingsgate Rd.
Columbus, Ohio 43221 U.S.A.

Phone: (614) 457-8504
Fax: (614) 457-4455

First Edition.....................1910
Second Edition. 1921
Third Edition. 1927
Fourth Edition.................. *1957*
Fifth Edition. *1963*
Sixth (Revised) Edition........ *1968*
Seventh Edition................ *1983*
Reprint...........................1987
Reprint...........................1996
Reprint...........................1998

ISBN 0-91-3321-34-6

Printed in Canada at Payette & Simms
300 Arran, St-Lambert, Que. J4R 1K5, Canada
by Ahmadiyya Anjuman Isha'at Islam, Lahore U.S.A.
1315 Kingsgate Rd.
Columbus, Ohio 43221 U.S.A.

CONTENTS

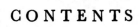

> "(O man), follow not that of which thou hast no knowledge" — 17 : 36.

ACKNOWLEDGEMENT

> "Say : O People of the Book, come to an equitable word between us and you, that we shall serve none but Allāh and that we shall not associate aught with Him, and that some of us shall not take others for lords beside Allāh . . . ! — 3 : 63.

This book, rendered into English by late Mawlāna Muḥammad 'Alī, was written by Ḥaḍrat Mirzā Ghulām Aḥmad under the title of *The Philosophy of the Teachings of Islam*; it was read at a religious conference held at Lahore in December 1896. It discusses from a Muslim's point of view the five subjects selected for discussion: (*i*) the physical, moral and spiritual conditions of man, (*ii*) the state of man in the life after death, (*iii*) the real object of the existence of man and means of its attainment, (*iv*) results produced by actions in the present life and the life to come, and (*v*) the sources of Divine knowledge.

The present treatise is primarily intended to be a messenger of goodwill between East and West.

The popularity it has so far enjoyed is shown by the fact that in the original Urdu form it has run into several editions. In the English language, it first appeared in instalments in the *Review of Religions* in 1902 when Mawlāna Muḥammad 'Alī was editing that paper. In book form, revised by Mr. Muḥammad A. Russel Webb, Mawlawī Sher 'Alī and Mr. Ghulām Muhammad, it was first published in 1910.

ABOUT THE AUTHOR

"Nay, whoever submits himself entirely to Allāh
and he is the doer of good (to others), he has
his reward from his Lord, and there is no fear
for such nor shall they grieve" — 2 : 112.

It was in the year 1835 that Ḥaḍrat Mirzā
Ghulām Aḥmad, son of Mirzā Ghulam Murtaḍā,
was born at Qadian, a village in the north of
Punjab. He belonged to a respectable Mughal
family, which traces its migration into India to
the time of Emperor Bābar, during the six-
teenth century.

He received his primary education in his
village. In his youth, though he loved solitude
and hated wordly pursuits, he was occupied, under
instructions of his father, in the management of
family lands. Again, to fulfil his father's wishes
in 1864, he joined government service at Sialkot.

It was here that the Mirza first came into contact with Christian missionaries.

In 1868, his father allowed him to give up service and to return to Qadian. For some years he was called upon to manage his family lands and to pursue law suits connected with them. He had to pay frequent visits to the town of Batala, which at that time was an important Christian district. He soon made up his mind to grapple with the unpleasant propaganda carried on by Christian missionaries against Islam.

After the death of his father in 1876, he devoted himself completely to the study of the Qur'ān, the Traditions and the Commentaries and the tenets of other religions. About that time, while he was refuting the Christian arguments against the Islamic doctrines, the Ārya Samāj Movement had started among the Hindus. In his controversies with its leaders, his scholarship and his enthusiasm to defend Islam came into display.

In 1880, appeared his famous book *Barāhīn-i Aḥmadiyyah*, which created a deep impression on Muslims in particular. In this first volume, he adduced a large number of arguments based on original texts, establishing the claims of Islam as the best religion for mankind. He emphasized the necessity of Divine inspiration and argued that God spoke to His chosen ones even today as He did in the past. In this connection, he referred to his own visions and inspirations and mentioned the fulfilment of some of these. In fact, it was while writing this book that it was revealed to him that he had been appointed the Reformer (*mujaddid*) of the fourteenth century of Hijrah for defending the cause of Islam.

In 1891, he announced that it had been revealed to him that Jesus Christ was not alive, but had died like other prophets. He declared that the Messiah, whose advent had been promised to the Muslims, was to be a Reformer of the nation and that the prophecies had been fulfilled in his own person. He further made it known that the reports relating to the appearance of the Mahdī also referred to the coming of the Messiah, who was to spread Islam in the world not by sword, but by argument and reasoning.

This statement raised against him a storm of opposition from Christians, Hindus as well as Muslims. However, in the midst of all trials and afflictions, with even the Government keeping strict watch over him owing to his claim to be the Mahdī, he continued propagating Islam with rare energy and sincerity. The burning passion of his heart was to carry the Message of Islam to the whole world, particularly to Europe, where only a dark picture of Islam had been drawn. His aspirations materialized to some extent in 1901, when he started an English monthly, the *Review of Religions*, from Qadian, to present a true picture of Islam and its Prophet to the English-knowing world. The plan was further developed after his death when at first, in 1912, the Woking Muslim Mission was established in England and later, in 1922, the German Muslim Mission at Berlin (West Germany). Thenceforward the task of propagating the teachings of Islam was carried from one country to another. Doubtless, the passion at the back of all this enterprise originated in the heart of that pious figure of Qadian, author of more than eighty books on Islam, who breathed his last on the 26th May, 1908.

PRELIMINARY NOTES

In the name of Allāh, the
Beneficent, the Merciful — 1:1.

Before I start with the proper subject, I may
state that all my assertions and arguments shall be
based upon and drawn from the Quran.[1] I deem
it a matter of the first importance that anybody,
who believes in any sacred scripture as the revealed
word of God, should so set limits to his advocacy
of the religion he supports as not to go out of the
Holy Book or depend upon arguments other than
those which it furnishes. For, if he does not observe
this rule in this auspicious meeting, he makes and
advances a new book and not the one which he
professes to support.

---

1. It may be noted that the author always used the word "Holy"
before Quran and Prophet Muḥammad (peace and blessings of God be on
him). In this publication, however, the word has been omitted to avoid
repetition — Publisher.

Therefore, as it is my object to show the beauties of the Quran and to establish its exclusive excellence over all other Books, I shall observe the rule above stated. As the other speakers are also expected to observe this rule, there will be a good opportunity for judicious minds to form a judgment as to the comparative merits of the various Books claiming to have been revealed. For the same reason, I shall avoid all reference to the authorities containing the reported sayings of Prophet Muḥammad, and shall not go outside the word of God as revealed in the Quran.

***

Some preliminary notes have been made at the outset which may appear as not bearing upon the questions. However, as they are necessary for the. full comprehension of the subject, I have been obliged to resort to them.

The first question relates to the physical, moral and spiritual conditions of man. The Quran observes this division by fixing three respective sources for this threefold condition of man, that is, three springs out of which these three conditions flow. The first of these in which the physical conditions of man take their birth is termed the *nafs al-ammāra*, which signifies the "uncontrollable spirit", or the "spirit prone to evil". Thus the Word of God says:

اِنَّ النَّفْسَ لَاَمَّارَةٌ بِالسُّوْءِ

"Surely (man's) self is wont to command (him to do) evil" — 12 : 53.

It is characteristic of the *nafs al-ammāra* that it inclines man to evil, tends to lead him into iniquitous and immoral paths, and stands in the way of his attainment of perfection and moral excellence. Man's nature is prone to evil and transgression at a certain stage in his development, and so long as he is devoid of high moral qualities, this evil nature is predominant in him. He is subject to this state so long as he does not walk in the light of true wisdom and knowledge, but acts in obedience to the natural inclinations of eating, drinking, sleeping, becoming angry or excited, just like the lower animals.

As soon, however, as he frees himself from the control of animal passions and, guided by reason and knowledge, he holds the reins of his natural desires and governs them instead of being governed by them — when a transformation is worked in his soul from grossness to virtue — he then passes out of the physical state and is a moral being in the strict sense of the word.

The source of the moral conditions of man is called, in the terminology of the Quran, the *nafs al-lawwāma*, or the "self-accusing soul":

وَلَاۤ اُقْسِمُ بِالنَّفْسِ اللَّوَّامَةِ ۞

"Nay, I swear by the self-accusing spirit!"[1] — 75 : 2.

This is the spring from which flows a highly moral life and, on reaching this stage, man is freed from bestiality. The swearing by the self-accusing soul indicates the regard in which it is held. For, the change from the disobedient to the self-accusing soul being a sure sign of its improvement and purification makes it deserving of approbation in the sight of the Almighty.

Lawwāma literally means "one who reproves severely", and the *nafs al-lawwāma* (self-accusing soul) has been so called because it upbraids a man for the doing of evil deeds and strongly hates upbridled passions and bestial appetites. Its tendency, on the other hand, is to generate noble qualities and a virtuous disposition, to transform life so as to bring the whole course and conduct of it to moderation, and to restrain the carnal passions and sensual desires so as to keep them within due bound.

Although, as stated above, the "self-accusing soul" upbraids itself for its faults and frailties, yet

---

1. That is, on every dereliction of duty or on the slightest act of disobedience, being conscious of having offended.

it is not the master of its passions, nor is it powerful enough to practise virtue exclusively. The weakness of the flesh has the upper hand sometimes, and then it stumbles and falls down. Its weakness then resembles that of a child who does not wish to fall but whose legs are sometimes unable to support him. It does not, however, persist in its fault, every failure bringing a fresh reproach. At this stage, the soul is anxious to attain moral excellence, and revolts against disobedience which is the characteristic of the first, or the animal stage, but does, notwithstanding its yearning for virtue, sometimes deviate from the line of duty.

The third or the last stage in the onward movement of the soul is reached on attaining to the source of all spiritual qualities. The soul at this stage is, in the words of the Quran, the *nafs al-mutma'inna*, or the "soul at rest":

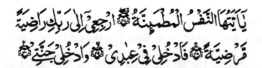

"O soul that art at rest, return to thy Lord, well-pleased, well-pleasing, so enter among My servants, and enter My Garden!" — 89: 27-30.

The soul is now freed from all weaknesses and frailties and is braced with spiritual strength. It is perfectly united with God and cannot live with-

out Him.   As water flows with great force down a
slope and, on account of its great mass and the total
absence of all obstacles, dashes down with irresistible force, so does the soul at this stage, casting off
all trammels, flow unrestrained towards its Maker.

It is further clear from the words "O soul that
art at rest with thy Lord, return to Him" that it is
in this life, and not after death, that this great
transformation is worked and that it is in this
world, and not elsewhere, that access to paradise is
granted to it.   Again, as the soul has been commanded to return to its Master, it is clear that
such a soul finds its support only in its Supporter.
The love of God is its food, and it drinks deep at
this fountain of life and is, therefore, delivered from
death.   The same idea is expressed elsewhere:

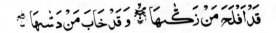

"He is indeed successful who causes it to grow,
and he indeed fails who buries it" — 91: 9-10.

In short, these three states of the soul may be
called the physical, the moral and the spiritual states
of man. Of these, the physical state — that in which
man seeks to satisfy the passions of the flesh — is
most dangerous when the passions run riot, for it
is then that they deal a death-blow to the moral
and spiritual qualities of man, and hence this state

has been termed the "disobedient spirit" in the Holy Word of God.

.*.

What is the effect of the teachings of the Quran upon the physical state of man, how does it guide us with respect to it, and what practical limits does it set to the natural inclinations?

It may be remarked at the outset that, according to the Muslim Scripture, the physical conditions of man are closely connected with his moral and spiritual states, so much so that even his modes of eating and drinking play a part in the moulding of his moral and spiritual qualities. If, therefore, his natural desires are subjected to the directions of the law, they take the form of moral qualities and deeply affect the spiritual state of the soul. It is for this reason that in all forms of devotion and prayer, and in all the injunctions relating to internal purity and moral rectitude, the greatest stress has been laid upon external purity and cleanliness and on the proper attitudes of the body.

The relation between the physical and spiritual natures of man would become evident on a careful consideration of the actions of the outward organs and the effect they produce upon the internal nature of man. Weeping, whether artificial, at once saddens the heart, while an artificial laugh makes it cheerful. Likewise, prostration of the body, as is done in prayer, causes the soul to humble itself and adore the Creator; whereas strutting stimulates vanity and vain glory.

Experience also shows the strong effect of good upon the heart and brain powers. For instance, the vegetarians ultimately lose all courage, and the result of giving up animal food is weakness of heart and loss of a noble quality. The same law is witnessed even among the animals. The herbivorous animals do not possess even a hundredth part of the courage of the carnivora, and the same may be said of birds. There is not the least doubt, then, that food plays an important part in the formation of character. Further, as actual exclusion of meat from diet causes certain deficiencies in the body of a person, so is excess of meat harmful to character for it would tend to suppress the qualities of humility and meekness. But those who adopt the middle path are heirs to both the noble qualities: courage and meekness. It is with this law in view that the Quran says:

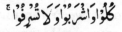

"(O children of Adam) eat and drink
and be not prodigal ... "[1] — 7: 31.

---

[1]. That is, in any particular form of diet so that one's character and health may not suffer from it.

The effect of the physical upon the moral nature of man has been spoken of, but it should also be noted that internal movements produce external actions. Grief brings tears into the eyes of a person and joy makes him laugh. Thus there is a natural relation between the body and the soul, and all the actions of the body such as eating, drinking, walking, sleeping, etc., necessarily produce a corresponding effect upon that which pertains to the state of the soul as distinguished from external actions. It is a well-known fact that a shock communicated to one point in the human brain causes loss of memory and, to another, brings about insensibility.

Air containing the poisonous germs of plague soon corrupts first the body and then the mind, and in a few hours the whole internal system in which reside the moral impulses is impaired and the unfortunate victim passes away. All this goes a long way to prove that there is a mysterious relation between the body and the soul of man and the solution of the mystery is undoubtedly beyond human comprehension.

Another argument is that the body itself is the mother of the soul The soul does not come from any place in the heavens and seek connection with the body in the womb of the mother, but it is, as it were, a light or an essence that lies concealed in the seed and grows with the growth of the body.

The Word of God gives us to understand that the
soul grows from the body while it is developed in
the womb of the mother:

ثُمَّ أَنْشَأْنَاهُ خَلْقًا اخَرَ فَتَبَارَكَ اللهُ أَحْسَنُ الْخَلِقِينَ ۞

"Then We cause it (life-germ) to grow
into another creation. So blessed be Allāh,
the Best of the creators !"[1] — 23 : 14.

The indication which the Quran has here
given us as to the nature of the connection between
the body and the soul leads us to other important
conclusions. It teaches us that the words which a
man speaks and the deeds which he does, if said or
done for the sake of God and to manifest His glory
and, if regulated by His commandments, are subject to the same Divine law: that in all the
outward actions there is a soul hidden as in the
seed of man, and as the body of these actions is
gradually developed, the hidden soul appears in it.
When the complete embodiment of the actions
takes place, the soul flashes suddenly in perfect
brightness and glory, and shows itself so far as the
spirit can be seen and there appears a plain movement of life. The full development of the body of
actions is followed by a blazing of the light within
like a flash of lightning. This stage is allegorically

---

1. This verse throws light on the nature of the soul and indicates the
strong and inexplicable tie between the soul and the body.

described in the following words of the Quran:

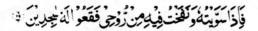

"So when I have made him (man) complete
and breathed into him of My spirit, fall
down making obeisance to him" — 15: 29.

This verse also suggests the same idea — that
on the complete embodiment of good action, the
spirit within brightens up. God describes this as
His own soul, thus indicating that it partakes of a
Divine nature. For, the body is fully developed
only after the extinction of the physical desires and,
consequently, the Divine light, which before was
dim, shines out in full lustre, and thus makes it
incumbent upon everybody to bow down before
the manifestation of this glory. Therefore, everyone is naturally attracted towards it and prostrates
before it, except the spirit of evil which loves
nothing but darkness.

To return to the subject, the soul is a light
which springs up from the body which is being
prepared in the womb. By the springing up of the
soul is only meant that at first it is hidden and
imperceptible, although its germs are present in the
seed itself, and that, as the body is gradually
developed, the soul grows along with it and becomes
manifest. There is no doubt that the inexplicable
relationship of the soul with the seed is in accor-

dance with the design of God and His will. It is a bright essence in the seed itself. It is not a part of it in the sense in which matter is part of matter, but at the same time it would be incorrect to say that it comes from outside or, as some wrongly imagine, falling upon the earth, it is mixed with the substance of the seed. It is hidden in the seed as fire is latent in the flint. The Word of God lends no support to the view that the soul comes from the heavens as something distinct from the body, or that it falls suddenly upon the earth and, mixing with the seed accidentally, finds an entrance into the womb. The idea is utterly false and totally opposed to the law of Nature.

The thousands of insects which can be observed daily in rotten articles of food or in unwashed wounds do not come from outside or descend from heaven. Their existence proves that the soul comes out of the body and is as surely a creation of God as anything else. From this, we conclude that the Almighty Who, with His wisdom and omnipotence, has created the soul out of the body, has willed and intended that a second birth of the soul should also be made manifest through the body. The movement of the soul depends upon that of the body, and if the body is drawn in any direction, the soul must follow. The physical state of man's life being of such great importance to the soul, the Word of God cannot be silent on the point. The Quran has, therefore, applied itself abundantly to the reformation of the physical state of man's life. It gives us the most valuable and minute directions on all matters of importance with which man is concerned: all his movements, the manner of the satisfaction of all his requirements, his family, social and general connections, health and sickness, are all regulated by laws and it is shown how external order and purity have their effect upon his spiritual state.

A few of the guiding rules will now be briefly noted, for, to describe them in detail would require much time. A close study of the Word of God on this important point — the injunctions and directions relating to the reformation of the external life of man and his gradual advancement from a state of barbarity to one of culture and then onward until he reaches the highest pinnacle of spiritual development — reveals the following all-wise method.

In the first place, God has been pleased to lead man out of darkness and raise him up from a savage state by teaching him the rules relating to his ordinary daily actions and mode of social life. Thus the process begins at the lowest points of man's development and, first of all, drawing a line of distinction between man and the lower animals, teaches him the elementary rules of morality which may pass under the name of social

behaviour.   Next, it undertakes to improve upon
this degree of morality by regulating man's
conduct and actions, thus turning them into sublime morals.   Both these methods relate only to
one stage of advancement, the difference being
only one of degree.   The Creator has so arranged
the system of moral evolution that one can
advance from a low state to a higher state.

We now come to the third stage of advancement when man completely forgets himself in the
love of God and in doing His will, and his whole
life is lived only for the sake of his Master.   This
is the stage to which the name *Islām* refers, for it
signifies total resignation to the will and service
of the Lord and total forgetfulness of self:

بَلَى مَنْ أَسْلَمَ وَجْهَهُ لِلَّهِ وَهُوَ مُحْسِنٌ فَلَهُ أَجْرُهُ
عِنْدَ رَبِّهِ وَلَا خَوْفٌ عَلَيْهِمْ وَلَا هُمْ يَحْزَنُونَ ۞

"Nay, whoever submits himself entirely to
Allāh and he is the doer of good (to others), he
has his reward from his Lord, and there is no
fear for such nor shall they grieve" — 2:112.

قُلْ إِنَّ صَلَاتِي وَنُسُكِي وَمَحْيَايَ وَمَمَاتِي لِلَّهِ رَبِّ الْعَالَمِينَ ۞
لَا شَرِيكَ لَهُ وَبِذَلِكَ أُمِرْتُ وَأَنَا أَوَّلُ الْمُسْلِمِينَ ۞

"(To the Prophet) Say: My prayer and my
sacrifice and my life and my death are surely

for Allāh, the Lord of the worlds—No associate
has He.   And this am I commanded, and I am
the first of those who submit'' — 6 : 163-164.

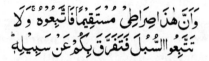

"And (know) that this is My path, the right one,
so follow it, and follow not (other) ways, for they
will lead you away from His way" — 6 : 154.

"Say : If you love Allāh, follow me: Allāh will
love you, and grant you protection from your
sins. And Allāh is Forgiving, Merciful" — 3: 30.

Before I deal with the three states of life, I
must repeat the caution that the physical state of
man's life, the dominant factor in which is the
"disobedient soul" cannot, according to the Word
of God, be treated as something quite distinct from
the moral state.   All the natural inclinations of
man and all the desires and passions of the
flesh have been placed by the Quran under
the heading of physical conditions.   These,
when operating under proper regulation and
co-ordination, are converted into excellent moral

qualities. Similarly, no hard and fast line can be drawn between the spheres of the moral and spiritual states. Man passes from one into the other after a total extinction of self in God, complete sanctification of the soul, entire severance from all low connections and thus achieving union with, unswerving loyalty to and extraordinary love of the Almighty and full submission to His will. One does not deserve the title of man so long as one's physical conditions are not in harmony with one's moral qualities, for the natural desires are common to man and the lower animals, and there is nothing to mark the distinction between them.

In the same manner, the mere possession of a few moral qualities does in no way bring about spiritual life. For instance, meekness of heart, peace of mind, and avoidance of mischief are only so many natural qualities which may be possessed even by a person who is quite ignorant of the significance of moral and spiritual values. Not a few animals are quite harmless and apparently free from savage tendencies. When tamed, they are not offensive in the least and, being lashed, do not resist. Yet it would be wrong to ascribe moral qualities to them. Likewise, persons who entertain the worst beliefs — nay, sometimes even those who otherwise are guilty of the blackest deeds — may possess such qualities.

It is possible for a person to be so tender-hearted as not to suffer the killing of the worms in his own wounds, intestines, or stomach. In some instances, tenderness of heart may induce a man to give up the use of honey or musk as the procuring of the one involves the dispersion and destruction of the bees, and that of the other the killing of the deer. There may even be persons so compassionate as to refrain from the use of pearls or silk, as both are obtained by the destruction of the life of worms. There also exist persons who would suffer severe pain rather than have leeches applied to them as the alleviation of the pain would be procured at the cost of the lives of these tiny worms. It is also possible that the feeling of tenderness may grow so strong in a person that he may even give up drinking of water, and thus put an end to his own life rather than destroy the animalcules contained in the water.

All this may be admitted, but would any reasonable person consider all such folly to be productive of any moral excellence or necessary to the state of a moral being? Is it thus that the soul of man can be purified of all internal corruptions which are obstacles in the way of the true realisation of God? Such harmlessness or inoffensiveness which is met with to a greater extent in some animals and birds than in man can never be the means of attaining to the desired degree of perfection. Nay, it is fighting with Nature and opposing its laws. It is rejecting the faculties and blessings with which we have been endowed. We cannot attain to spiritual perfection unless we bring into play the various faculties in their proper place as occasion may require, and walk with perseverance in the path which God has pointed out to us, submitting ourselves wholly to His will.

As already stated, there are three factors which give rise to the threefold nature of man: the disobedient soul, the self-accusing soul and the soul at rest. Accordingly, there are three stages of reformation corresponding to these three factors. In the first stage, we are concerned with mere ignorant savages whom it is our duty to raise to the status of civilized beings, by teaching them the social laws regulating their mutual relations. The first step, therefore, consist in teaching the savage not to walk about naked, or devour carcasses, or indulge in other barbarous habits. This is the lowest stage in the reformation of man. In humanizing people upon whom no ray of the light of civilization has yet fallen, it is necessary, first of all, to take them through this stage and make them accustomed to elementary rules of morality.

When the savage has learnt the rudiments of society, he is prepared for the second stage of reformation. He is then taught the high excellent moral qualities pertaining to humanity as well as the proper use of his own faculties, and of what lies hidden beneath them.

Those who have acquired excellent morals are then prepared for the third stage and, after they have attained to outward perfection, they taste of union with, and the love of God.

These are the three stages which the Quran has prescribed for a wayfarer who desires to travel along the path that leads to the Creator.

* * *

Attention must also be called to another very important point. The Quran does not inculcate doctrines which are contrary to reason and which, therefore, a person can follow only against his better judgment. The whole purpose of the Book, and the pith of its teachings, is the threefold reformation of man, and all other directions are simply means to this end. As is seen in the treatment of bodily diseases, the physician recognizes the necessity of dissecting or performing surgical operations or applying ointments to wounds, etc. The Quran also employs these means on fit occasions to serve the purpose when necessary and advisable. All its moral teachings, precepts and doctrines have an all-pervading purpose beneath them which consists in transforming men from the physical state, which is imbued with a tinge of savageness, into the moral state, and from the moral into the spiritual state, which is boundless.

It has already been observed that physical conditions of man do not differ in quality from his moral state. The fact is that physical conditions, when subjected to regulation and used within proper limits according to the directions of reason and good judgment, are transformed into moral conditions. Before a man is guided in his actions by the dictates of reason and conscience, his acts do not at all fall under the heading of moral conditions however much they may resemble them; they are but natural and instinctive impulses. For instance, the affection and docility which a dog or a cat or any other domestic animal shows towards its master cannot be designated as courtesy or refined manners, nor can the fierceness of a lion or a wolf be classed as rudeness or misbehaviour. What we call good or ill manners or morals are the results of the exercise of reason that comes into play on appropriate occasions. A man who is not guided by the dictates of reason in his actions may be compared either to a child whose reasoning powers are not yet matured or to an insane who has lost all reason. The only line of distinction that can be drawn between the movements of a madman or a child, on the one hand, and the actions of a man of reason, on the other, is that the former are only natural impulses while the latter are the result of an exercise of the reasoning faculty. For instance, the child will, as soon as it is born, seek the breast of its mother, while a chicken will, after it is hatched, begin to pick up food with its beak. Similarly, a leech inherits instinctively the habits of that worm and a serpent or a lion the habits of its own kind.

The child begins, soon after its birth, to show human peculiarities. As it advances in years, these become more conspicuous. It cries louder and its smile develops into laughter. It expresses its pleasure or displeasure in its movements, but these movements are still more the result of impulse than of an exercise of the intellect. Such is also man in his savage state when his intellectual faculties are yet in an embryonic state. He is subject to the impulses of his nature and whatever he does, he does in obedience to them. His deeds are not the result of due deliberation. The impulses of his nature, subject to external conditions, take an outward shape.

It should not, however, be assumed that all these movements are necessarily improper; some of them may resemble the deliberate acts of a reasonable person, but it cannot be denied that they are not preceded by any exercise of the reasoning faculties or by any deep consideration of their propriety or impropriety. Even if we assume the presence of a slight degree of reasoning in some acts of the savage, we cannot class them generally as good or bad actions, for the more powerful factor in bringing them about is not the reasoning faculty but an instinctive impulse or a yielding to desire and passion.

In short, we cannot class as "moral" the acts of a person whose life is akin to that of the savage and who is subject to his natural impulses like the lower animals, infants or madmen. The first stage of a moral being — of one whose acts can be classed as good or bad morally — is that in which he is capable of distinguishing between good and bad actions, or between two good or two bad actions of different degrees. This takes place when the reasoning faculty is sufficiently well developed to form general ideas and perceive the remoter consequences of actions. It is then that man regrets the omission of a good deed or feels repentance or remorse after doing a bad one. This is the second stage of man's life which the Quran calls *nafs al-lawwama*, "self-accusing soul" or, to take a more familiar term, "conscience".

But it should be remembered that, for the savage to attain to this stage of the self-accusing soul, mere admonition is not sufficient. He must have so much knowledge of God that he should not look upon his own creation by the Almighty as an insignificant or meaningless act. This soul-ennobling perception of the Lord can alone lead to actions truly moral, and it is for this reason that the Quran inculcates a true knowledge of God along with its admonitions and warnings and assures man that every good or bad action bears fruit which may cause spiritual bliss or torture in this life, while a clearer and more palpable reward or punishment awaits him in the next.

In other words, when man reaches this stage of advancement, called the "self-accusing soul", his reason, knowledge and conscience reach the stage of development in which a feeling of remorse overtakes him in the doing of unrighteous deeds and he becomes eager to perform good ones. This is the stage in which the actions of man can be said to be moral.

It seems necessary here to define the word _khulq_ (moral). There are two words alike in form except in the vowel point: _khalq_ which signifies "external creation" and _khulq_, meaning "internal creation" (or inborn quality). As the perfection of internal creation is achieved through moral excellence and not through the innate passions of man, the former is the proper signifi-cance of the word _khalq_, and not the latter. We may take this opportunity of exposing the error of the popular view that forbearance, humility, meekness and the like are the only qualities which constitute good morals. The fact is that, corresponding to every external action, there is an inner quality which, when exercised in its proper place, is termed "moral". For instance, in weeping the outward action is that of the eye from which tears flow, but corresponding to this there is in the heart a quality of melting which may be called "tenderness" which, when properly applied by a moral being, is one of the excellent morals.

Again, a man uses his hands in defending himself against, or opposing, an enemy, but corresponding to this power of the external organ, there is in the heart a quality which we call "courage" and this, when properly used, is also one of the high morals, the possession of which is necessary for man to attain perfection. Similarly, a man sometimes saves an oppressed person from the oppressor with his hands or feels impelled to give something to the helpless or the hungry or serve mankind in some other way. All such actions proceed from the inner quality, which is called "commiseration". Or, sometimes, a person inflicts punishment upon a wrongdoer and the source of this outward action is the moral quality termed "vengeance". Or, again, there are occasions upon which a man who receives an injury, refrains from injuring in return, and he passes over the action of the aggressor. This refraining results from the moral quality, called "forbearance". In like manner, man sometimes employs his hands or feet or brain or wealth in doing good to his fellow-beings. In such cases the corresponding moral quality is "charity". The truth is, as already stated, that all these qualities are only ranked as moral qualities when they are used on the proper occasion. Thus, in the Holy Book, addressing Prophet Muḥammad, the Supreme Being says:

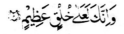

"And surely thou hast sublime morals"[1] — 68 : 4.

In short, all the qualities with which man's mind is naturally endowed, such as politeness, modesty, honesty, generosity, jealousy, perseverance, chastity, devoutness, moderation, compassion, sympathy, courage, charity, forgiveness, patience, kindness, truth, fidelity, etc., when they are called into action within their proper spheres and on proper occasions, fall under the definition of virtue. All these grow out of the natural inclinations and passions of man when the latter are controlled and regulated by reason. The desire for progress is an essential characteristic of man and is not shared by the lower animals. Hence

---

1. This means that all the high moral qualities such as charity, courage, justice, mercy, kindness, truth, high-mindedness, etc., are combined in the Prophet's person.

it is that true religion, good company and virtuous injunctions transform man's natural inclinations into morals.

.*.

Prophet Muḥammad's advent took place at a time when the whole world had sunk to the lowest depths of ignorance. To this, the Quran refers in the following words:

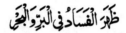

"Corruption has appeared in the land and the sea . . ." — 30 : 41.

The metaphorical phrase translated into plain language would mean that the "people who had been given the Scriptures from God" (*Ahl al-Kitāb*) had become corrupt as well as those who had ever drunk of the fountain of Inspiration. The Quran was, therefore, sent to bring life to the dead:

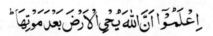

"Know that Allāh gives life to the earth after its death . . ." — 57 : 17.

Utter darkness and barbarism at that time prevailed over the whole of Arabia. No social laws were observed, and the most despicable deeds were openly committed. An unlimited number of wives was taken, and all prohibited things were made lawful. Rapine and incest raged unchecked and, not infrequently, mothers were taken for wives. It was to prohibit this horrible custom that these words were revealed:

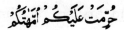

"Forbidden to you are your mothers . . ." — 4: 23.

Like beasts, the people did not even hesitate to devour carcasses, and cannibalism was not unknown. There was no vice which was not freely practised by them. The great majority of these people did not believe in a future life, and not a few were atheists. Infanticide prevailed throughout the country, and they mercilessly killed orphans to rob them of their properties. To the outward eye, they had the forms of men, but they were totally devoid of rationality, modesty, jealousy and other manly qualities. Their thirst for wine was excessive and fornication was committed unscrupulously. Ignorance prevailed so widely that the neighbouring people called them the "ignorant" (ummī).

Such is the dark picture of the time and the country in which the Prophet of Islam appeared, and it was to reclaim such wild and ignorant people that the Word of God came upon him. The threefold reformation of man to which

attention has been called was, therefore, destined
to be brought about at that period by means of
the Quran. It is for this reason that the Holy Book
claims to be a perfect guidance for mankind as to
it alone was given the opportunity to work a reformation complete in all respects. It had a grand aim
before it. It had first to reclaim mankind from
savagery and to make them men, then to teach
them excellent morals and make them good men
and, finally, to take them to the highest pinnacles
of advancement and make them godly.

THE THREE CONDITIONS OF MAN

"And those who strive hard for Us, We shall certainly guide them in Our ways. And Allāh is surely with the doers of good" — 29 : 69.

We shall now consider the teachings of the Holy Book relating to the first stage of the threefold reformation — physical, moral and spiritual conditions of man — which we have referred to in the foregoing pages.

A. PHYSICAL CONDITIONS

Laws are laid down to guide the actions of daily life, and all that is necessary to make the savage a social being is included therein. This is the earliest stage in man's civilization and it teaches that particular aspect of morals which we term *'adab* (manners).

Marriage

We shall first examine the question of marriage as inculcated in the Holy Quran:

وَلَاتَنْكِحُوامَانَكَحَ اٰبَاؤُكُمْ مِّنَ النِّسَاءِ اِلَّامَاقَدْ سَلَفَ

"(O you who believe) and marry not (those) women whom your fathers married, except what has already passed (of that nature)" — 4 : 22.

حُرِّمَتْ عَلَيْكُمْ اُمَّهٰتُكُمْ وَبَنٰتُكُمْ وَاَخَوٰتُكُمْ وَعَمّٰتُكُمْ وَخٰلٰتُكُمْ وَبَنٰتُ الْاَخِ وَبَنٰتُ الْاُخْتِ وَاُمَّهٰتُكُمُ الّٰتِیْۤ اَرْضَعْنَكُمْ وَاَخَوٰتُكُمْ مِّنَ الرَّضَاعَةِ وَاُمَّهٰتُ نِسَآئِكُمْ وَرَبَآئِبُكُمُ الّٰتِیْ فِیْ حُجُوْرِكُمْ مِّنْ نِّسَآئِكُمُ الّٰتِیْ دَخَلْتُمْ بِهِنَّ فَاِنْ لَّمْ تَكُوْنُوْا دَخَلْتُمْ بِهِنَّ فَلَاجُنَاحَ عَلَيْكُمْ وَحَلَآئِلُ اَبْنَآئِكُمُ الَّذِيْنَ مِنْ اَصْلَابِكُمْ وَاَنْ تَجْمَعُوْا بَيْنَ الْاُخْتَيْنِ اِلَّامَاقَدْ سَلَفَ

"Forbidden to you are your mothers, and your daughters, and your sisters, and your paternal and maternal aunts, and brother's daughters and sister's daughters, and your mothers that have suckled you, and your foster-sisters, and mothers-in-law, and your step-daughters who are in your guardianship (born) of your wives to whom you have gone in — but if you have not gone in to them, there is no blame on you — and the wives of your sons who are of your own

loins; and that you should have two sisters
together, except what has passed. . ."— 4 : 23.

وَإِنْ خِفْتُمْ أَلَّا تُقْسِطُوا فِى الْيَتَىٰ فَانكِحُوا مَا طَابَ
لَكُم مِّنَ النِّسَاءِ مَثْنَىٰ وَثُلَثَ وَرُبَعَ فَإِنْ خِفْتُمْ
أَلَّا تَعْدِلُوا فَوَاحِدَةً أَوْ مَا مَلَكَتْ

"And if you fear that you cannot do justice to
orphans, marry such women as seem good to you,
two, or three, or four; but if you fear that you
will not do justice, then (marry) only one or
that which your right hands possess . . ."[1]— 4 : 3

ٱلْيَوْمَ أُحِلَّ لَكُمُ الطَّيِّبَتُ وَطَعَامُ الَّذِينَ أُوتُوا الْكِتَبَ حِلٌّ
لَّكُمْ وَطَعَامُكُمْ حِلٌّ لَّهُمْ وَالْمُحْصَنَتُ مِنَ الْمُؤْمِنَتِ وَ
الْمُحْصَنَتُ مِنَ الَّذِينَ أُوتُوا الْكِتَبَ مِن قَبْلِكُمْ إِذَا آتَيْتُمُوهُنَّ
أُجُورَهُنَّ مُحْصِنِينَ غَيْرَ مُسَفِحِينَ وَلَا مُتَّخِذِى أَخْدَانٍ

"This day (all) good things are made lawful for
you. And the food of those who have been
given the Book is lawful for you and your food
is lawful for them. And so are the chaste from
among the believing women and the chaste from

---

1. There is no harm in your marrying the orphan girls who are your
wards, but if you are apprehensive that, as they have no guardian besides
yourselves, you may be sometimes tempted to deal with them
unjustly, then marry of other women who have guardians : two, three
or four, provided you can act equitably towards them in all respects.

among those who have been given the Book
before you, when you give them their dowries,
taking (them) in marriage, not fornicating nor
taking them for paramours in secret . . ."[1] — 5:5.

وَأَتُوا النِّسَآءَ صَدُقَاتِهِنَّ نِحْلَةً

"And give women (whom you take in marriage)
their dowries as a free gift . . . " — 4 : 4.

يَا يُّهَا الَّذِيْنَ اٰمَنُوا لَا يَحِلُّ لَكُمْ اَنْ تَرِثُوا النِّسَآءَ كَرْهًا

"O you who believe, it is not lawful for you to
inherit women against (their) will . . . " — 4: 19.

Moral

The practice of burying female infants was
universal in the pre-Islamic period. And the
Holy Quran forbids this atrocious act in the
following unambiguous words :

وَلَا تَقْتُلُوْا اَوْلَادَكُمْ

"And slay not your children . . ." — 6: 152.

وَلَا تَقْتُلُوْا اَنْفُسَكُمْ

"And kill not your people . . . " — 4 : 29.

---

1. There was a custom among some ignorant Arabs that, if children
were not born to a man, his wife would secretly go to another man for
getting issues. It is for the extirpation of this savage custom that these
words have been used.

Food, alcohol, gambling

Like beasts, the Arabs did not hesitate to devour carcasses. Their thirst for wine was excessive, and gambling was not unknown. It is to rectify such low practices that the following verses were revealed:

حُرِّمَتْ عَلَيْكُمُ الْمَيْتَةُ وَالدَّمُ وَلَحْمُ الْخِنْزِيرِ وَمَآ أُهِلَّ لِغَيْرِ
اللهِ بِهِ وَالْمُنْخَنِقَةُ وَالْمَوْقُوذَةُ وَالْمُتَرَدِّيَةُ وَالنَّطِيحَةُ وَ
مَآ أَكَلَ السَّبُعُ إِلَّا مَاذَكَّيْتُمْ وَمَاذُبِحَ عَلَى النُّصُبِ

"Forbidden to you is that which dies of itself, and blood, and flesh of swine,[1] and that on which any other name than that of Allāh has been invoked, and the strangled (animal), and that beaten to death, and that killed by a fall, and that killed by goring with the horn, and that

---

1. *Khinzir* (swine), mentioned in this verse, is one of those things which the Muslims have been forbidden to eat. The very name of this foul animal contains an allusion to the prohibition of its flesh. It is a combination of *khinz* and *ar*, the first part meaning "very foul" and the second "I see". The word literally means: "I see it very foul". The name which God gave this animal in the beginning, therefore, points to its foulness. It is yet more interesting to note that in Hindi this animal is known by the name of *sū'ar* which is composed of two words *sū* and *'ar* the latter part being identical with the Arabic word and the former being the exact equivalent of the first part of the Arabic form. The Hindi word thus means exactly the same as the Arabic. The Arabic origin of a Hindi word is not surprising for, as shown in my book *Minān al-Raḥmān*, Arabic is the mother of all languages and its words are frequently met with in all languages. *Sū'ar* is, therefore, of Arabic ethnology.

In Hindi, this animal is also known as *bad*, meaning "bad" or "foul", which is probably a translation of the original Arabic word. It appears that at an early age in the world's history, when separation had taken place, the word *sū'ar* which is the exact equivalent of, and synonymous with the still-prevalent Arabic form *khinzir*, was used to signify the name

which wild beasts have eaten — except what
you slaughter ; and that which is sacrificed
on stones set up (for idols) . . ." — 5: 3.

كُلُواْ وَاشْرَبُواْ وَلَا تُسْرِفُوٓاْ

"Eat and drink but be not prodigal"— 7:31.

يَسْئَلُونَكَ مَاذَآ أُحِلَّ لَهُمْ قُلْ أُحِلَّ لَكُمُ الطَّيِّبَتُ

"They ask thee (the Prophet Muḥammad)
as to what is allowed to them. Say: The
good things are allowed to you . . . " — 5: 4.

إِنَّمَا الْخَمْرُ وَالْمَيْسِرُ وَالْأَنْصَابُ وَالْأَزْلَامُ رِجْسٌ
مِنْ عَمَلِ الشَّيْطَنِ فَاجْتَنِبُوهُ لَعَلَّكُمْ تُفْلِحُونَ

"Intoxicants and games of chance and (sacrificing to) stones set up and (dividing by) arrows

---

of this animal, and it has kept the original form after a lapse of
thousands of years. The Sanskrit form of the word may have changed a
little, but there can be no doubt that the root is Arabic, for it supplies
the reason for which the name was given, and the word *khinzir* attests
to the truth of the same view.

As to the applicability of this sense of the word to the habits of this
animal, there can be no question. Everybody knows that it is extremely
ugly and lives upon filth and is, moreover, the most shameless of all
creatures. The reason of its prohibition is thus evident. Taken as food
its foul flesh will have an injurious effect upon the body as well as the soul,
for we have shown above that food affects the whole external and internal
system of man. It may be recalled that pre-Islamic physicians of the
Greek school also held that the flesh of this animal was injurious.

On similar grounds, the Quran has prohibited the flesh of animals that
die a natural death, for it also affects both physical health and morals.
Animals, strangled or killed by a blow, are treated like those that
die a natural death.

are only an uncleanness, the devil's work ;
so shun it that you may succeed"[1] — 5 : 90.

$$ \text{وَتَزَوَّدُوْا فَإِنَّ خَيْرَ الزَّادِ التَّقْوٰى} $$

"And make provision for yourselves, the best
provision being to keep one's duty . . ." — 2:197

$$ \text{وَفِىْ أَمْوَالِهِمْ حَقٌّ لِّلسَّآئِلِ وَالْمَحْرُوْمِ} $$

"In their wealth there was a due share for the
beggar and for one who is denied good" —'51 :19.

Manners

With regard to social behaviour, the Quran
teaches us the following:

$$ \text{لَا تَدْخُلُوْا بُيُوْتًا غَيْرَ بُيُوْتِكُمْ حَتّٰى تَسْتَأْنِسُوْا وَتُسَلِّمُوْا} $$
$$ \text{عَلٰٓى أَهْلِهَا ذٰلِكُمْ خَيْرٌ لَّكُمْ لَعَلَّكُمْ تَذَكَّرُوْنَ فَإِنْ} $$
$$ \text{لَّمْ تَجِدُوْا فِيْهَآ أَحَدًا فَلَا تَدْخُلُوْهَا حَتّٰى يُؤْذَنَ لَكُمْ} $$
$$ \text{وَإِنْ قِيْلَ لَكُمُ ارْجِعُوْا فَارْجِعُوْا هُوَ أَزْكٰى لَكُمْ} $$

"(O you who believe) enter not houses other than
your own houses, until you have asked permission
and saluted their inmates. This is better for you
that you may be mindful. But if you find no one
therein, enter them not, until permission is given

---

1. Never in the history of the world were such deep-rooted evils as
intoxicants and games of chance so suddenly eradicated with the
dvent of Islam — Publisher.

to you; and if it is said to you, Go back, then
go back; this is purer for you" — 24: 27-28.

وَأْتُوا الْبُيُوتَ مِنْ أَبْوَابِهَا

"And go into the houses by their doors"[1] — 2:189.

قُولُوا قَوْلًا سَدِيدًا

"(O you who believe, keep your duty to
Allāh and) speak straight words"[2] — 33:70.

وَاقْصِدْ فِي مَشْيِكَ وَاغْضُضْ مِنْ صَوْتِكَ

"And pursue the right course in thy going
about and lower thy voice . . ." — 31: 19.

وَإِذَا حُيِّيتُمْ بِتَحِيَّةٍ فَحَيُّوا بِأَحْسَنَ مِنْهَا أَوْ رُدُّوهَا

"And when you are greeted with a greeting, greet
with one better than it, or return it . . ." — 4:86.

إِذَا قِيلَ لَكُمْ تَفَسَّحُوا فِي الْمَجَالِسِ فَافْسَحُوا
يَفْسَحِ اللَّهُ لَكُمْ وَإِذَا قِيلَ انْشُزُوا فَانْشُزُوا

"(O you who believe) when it is said to you,
make room in assemblies, make room. Allāh
will give you ample (hereafter). And when
it is said, Rise up, rise up . . ." — 58: 11.

----

1. That is, do not jump over the walls, nor enter by the back-door.
2. That is, do not indulge in idle talk, but speak rightly when
occasion requires it.

Hygiene

The Holy Quran teaches us to keep our body clean, and to wash ourselves in case we are under an obligation:

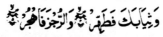

"(O you who believe) if you are under an obligation, then wash (yourselves) . . ." — 5: 6.

وَثِيَابَكَ فَطَهِّرْ ۝ وَالرُّجْزَ فَاهْجُرْ ۝

"And thy garments do purify, and (every kind of) uncleanness do shun . . ." — 74: 4-5.

This is the primary step which the Quran has taken for the reformation of man and those are the rules by means of which it has, in the past, raised, and claims now to raise, savages to the status of social beings. These teachings simply contain rules of good conduct and social relations. So far it does not inculcate teachings containing high morals which are intended to make men morally great. It was necessary that this step should have first been taken for people whose regeneration was the primary object of our Prophet's appearance and who were actually living in a state of savagery far surpassing that of other peoples. They observed no law which could differentiate them from savages. It was, therefore, necessary that

the Holy Book should have first of all taught
them the rules of society.

B. Moral Conditions

After giving the savage the necessary rules of
guidance, the Quran undertakes to teach him
high morals. We shall mention, by way of illustration, only a few of the moral qualities upon which
stress has been laid.

All moral qualities fall under two heads: firstly,
those which enable a man to abstain from inflicting
injury upon his fellow-men, and, secondly, those
which enable him to do good to others. To the
first class belong the rules which direct the inten-
tions and actions of man so that he may not injure
the life, property or honour of his fellow-beings
through his tongue or hand or eye or any other
member of his body. The second class comprises
all rules calculated to guide the motives and
actions of man for doing good to others by means
of the faculties which God has granted him, or in
declaring the glory or honour of others, or in
forbearing from a punishment which an offender
deserves, thus giving him the positive benefit of
having escaped a physical punishment or loss of
property which he would otherwise have suffered,
or in punishing him in such a manner that the
punishment turns out to be a blessing for him.

Chastity

The moral qualities which fall under the heading of abstaining from injuries are four in number. Each one of these is designated by a single word in the Arabic language whose rich vocabulary supplies an appropriate word for different human conceptions, manners and morals.

First of all, let us consider *ihsān* or "chastity". This word signifies the virtue which relates to the act of procreation in a person. A man or a woman is said to be *muhsin* or *muhsina* when he or she abstains from illegal intercourse and its preliminaries which bring disgrace and ruin upon the head of the sinners in this world and severe torture in the next, besides the disgrace and loss caused to those connected with them. None is more wicked than the infamous villain who causes the loss of a wife to a husband and of a mother to her children, and thus violently disturbs the peace of a household, bringing ruin upon the head of both, the guilty wife and the innocent husband, not to talk of the children.

The first thing to remember about this priceless moral quality, called "chastity", is that no one deserves credit for refraining from satisfying his carnal desires illegally, if nature has not granted him those desires. The words "moral quality" therefore cannot be applied to the mere act of refraining from such a course unless nature has also made a man capable of committing the evil deed. It is refraining under such circumstances — against the power of the passions which nature has placed in man — that deserves to be credited as a high moral quality. Nonage, impotency, emasculation or old age nullify the existence of the moral quality we term "chastity", although a refraining from the illegal act exists in these cases. But the fact is that in such cases it is a natural condition, and there is no resistance of passion, and consequently no propriety or impropriety is involved.

This, as has already been said, is an important distinction between natural conditions and moral qualities. In the former there is no tendency to go to the opposite direction, while in the latter there exists a struggle between the good and evil passions which necessitates the application of the reasoning faculty.

There is no doubt then that, as indicated in the foregoing pages, children under the age of puberty and men who have lost the power upon which restrictions are to be imposed, cannot claim to possess a moral quality of so great a value, though their actions might resemble chastity. It is only a natural condition over which they have absolutely no control. The directions contained in the Holy Book for the attainment of this noble quality are described in the following words:

وَلْيَسْتَعْفِفِ الَّذِينَ لَا يَجِدُونَ نِكَاحًا

"(Allāh is knowing) and let those who cannot find a match keep chaste..."[1] — 24 : 33.

وَلَا تَقْرَبُوا الزِّنَى إِنَّهُ كَانَ فَاحِشَةً وَسَاءَ سَبِيلًا ۝

"And go not nigh to fornication: surely it is an obscenity. And evil is the way" — 17 : 32.

قُلْ لِلْمُؤْمِنِينَ يَغُضُّوا مِنْ أَبْصَارِهِمْ وَيَحْفَظُوا فُرُوجَهُمْ
ذَٰلِكَ أَزْكَىٰ لَهُمْ إِنَّ اللَّهَ خَبِيرٌ بِمَا يَصْنَعُونَ ۝ وَقُلْ لِلْمُؤْمِنَاتِ
يَغْضُضْنَ مِنْ أَبْصَارِهِنَّ وَيَحْفَظْنَ فُرُوجَهُنَّ وَلَا يُبْدِينَ
زِينَتَهُنَّ إِلَّا مَا ظَهَرَ مِنْهَا وَلْيَضْرِبْنَ بِخُمُرِهِنَّ عَلَىٰ جُيُوبِهِنَّ
وَلَا يَضْرِبْنَ بِأَرْجُلِهِنَّ لِيُعْلَمَ مَا يُخْفِينَ مِنْ زِينَتِهِنَّ ۚ
تُوبُوا إِلَى اللَّهِ جَمِيعًا أَيُّهَ الْمُؤْمِنُونَ لَعَلَّكُمْ تُفْلِحُونَ ۝

"Say to the believing men that they lower their gaze and restrain their sexual passions. That is purer for them. Surely Allāh is aware of what they do. And say to the believing women that they lower their gaze and restrain their sexual passions and do not display their adorn-

---

1. Other means to preserve one's continence can be employed: fasting or taking light food or doing hard work. However, some people have devised methods of their own for refraining themselves from sexual relations as by adopting celibacy or monasticism and thus deprecating marriage, or by submitting themselves to castration.

ment except what appears thereof. And let them wear their head-coverings over their bosoms. And they should not display their adornment except to their husbands or their fathers, or the fathers of their husbands, or their sons, or the sons of their husbands, or their brothers, or their brothers' sons, or their sisters' sons, or their women, or those whom their right hands possess, or guileless male servants, or the children who know not women's nakedness. And let them not strike their feet so that the adornment that they hide may be known. And turn to Allāh all, O believers, so that you may be successful" — 24: 30-31.

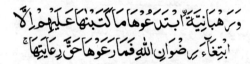

"And (as for) monkery they innovated it — We did not prescribe it to them — only to seek Allāh's pleasure, but they did not observe it with its due observance . . ."1 — 57 : 27.

---

1. Here, God negatives the assertion of His having prescribed the methods of castration, etc., for, had these been the commandments of the Lord, all the people would have had to observe these rules and then the human race would long since have disappeared from the face of the earth. In addition to the disadvantages and immorality attaching to this practice, it is an objection against the Creator for having created such a power in man. Moreover, it can be readily seen that there is no merit in being unable to do an act. Credit is due to him only who resists the evil tendency and overcomes the evil passions out of fear of God. The person who has the capacity deserves a twofold credit: for its exercise in the proper place and for refraining from applying it where it is not the proper occasion. But the man who has lost the capacity is not entitled to either one of these. He is like a child and deserves no credit for refraining from what he has lost the power to do. There is no resistance, no overcoming and, consequently, no merit whatsoever.

These verses not only contain excellent teachings for the preservation of chastity but also point out five remedies for observing continence: restraining the eyes from looking upon strangers, and the ears from hearing voices exciting lust, or hearing the love-stories of others, avoiding every occasion where there may be risk of being involved in the wicked deed and, last of all, fasting, etc., in case of celibacy. We can confidently assert that the excellent teachings on chastity, together with the remedies for continence, as contained in the Holy Book, are a peculiarity of Islam.

One particular point deserves special attention here : the natural propensity of man, in which sexual appetite takes its roots and over which man cannot have full control except by undergoing a thorough transformation is that, whenever there is an occasion for it, it flares up and throws him into serious danger. The Divine injunction in this respect is, therefore, not that we may look upon strange women and their beauty and ornaments or their gait and dancing so long as we do it with pure intent nor that it is lawful for us to listen to their sweet songs or to the stories of their love and beauty, provided it is done with a pure heart, but that it is not lawful for us to cast glances at them whether with a pure or an impure heart. We are forbidden to do an act in the doing of which we are not treading upon sure ground. We must avoid every circumstance which might make us stumble. Unrestrained looks are sure to lead one into danger and, therefore, it is prohibited for us not only to look at a woman lustfully but not to look at her at all so that the eye and the heart should remain pure and secure against temptation.

For the attainment and preservation of chastity, therefore, there could be no higher teaching and no nobler doctrine than that inculcated by the Holy Quran. The Word of God restrains the carnal desires of man even from smouldering in secret and enjoins upon him to avoid the very occasions where there is danger of excitement of evil passions.

This is the secret underlying the principle of the seclusion of women in Islam. It is sheer ignorance of the noble principles of this religion to suggest that seclusion means shutting up women like prisoners in gaol. The object of seclusion is to restrain both men and women from intermingling freely, and that neither sex should be at liberty to display its decoration and beauty to the other sex. This excellent rule is conducive to the good of both sexes.[1]

---

1. Note that *ghaz baṣar* in Arabic means the casting down of one's eyes when the object in view is not one which it is proper for a person to look at freely, and not the restraining of one's looks on the proper occasion. A person who is yearning after righteousness of heart should not be looking on all sides. The casting down of eyes on proper occasions is the first requirement of social life. The habit, without causing any disadvantage to man in his social relation, has the invaluable advantage of making him perfect in one of the highest morals called "chastity".

Honesty

We come next to the second moral quality of refraining from injury, which is called in Arabic *amānat* or "honesty". This consists in not injuring others by deceiving them or taking unlawful possession of their properties. This quality is naturally met with in man. An infant, free as it is from every bad habit, is averse to sucking the milk of a woman other than its mother if it has not been entrusted to her when quite unconscious. This habit in the infant is the root from which flows the natural inclination to be honest, which is later developed into the moral quality known as "honesty".

The true principle of honesty is that there should be the same aversion of the dishonest taking of another's property as the child has to sucking the milk of a woman who is not its mother. In the child, however, this is not a moral quality but only a natural impulse, inasmuch as it is not regulated by any principle or displayed on the proper occasion. The child has no choice in the matter and, unless there is a choice, the action, not being the action of a moral being, cannot be included in the category of moral condition.

A man who, like the child, shows this inclination in obedience to the requirements of his nature without looking to the propriety of the occasion cannot, in the strict sense of the word, be called

an honest and faithful person. He who does not
strictly observe the conditions which raise this
natural inclination to the status of a moral quality
cannot lay any claim to it, although his action
might, to outward appearance, resemble that of a
moral being which is done with all the requisites
and after a due consideration of its advisability.
In illustration, a few verses from the Holy Quran
may be quoted here:

وَلَا تُؤْتُوا السُّفَهَآءَ أَمْوَالَكُمُ الَّتِى جَعَلَ اللهُ لَكُمْ قِيَامًا وَارْزُقُوهُمْ
فِيهَا وَاكْسُوهُمْ وَقُولُوا لَهُمْ قَوْلًا مَعْرُوفًا ۞ وَابْتَلُوا
الْيَتَامَى حَتَّى اِذَا بَلَغُوا النِّكَاحَ فَاِنْ اَنَسْتُمْ مِنْهُمْ رُشْدًا فَادْفَعُوا
اِلَيْهِمْ اَمْوَالَهُمْ وَلَا تَاْكُلُوهَا اِسْرَافًا وَبِدَارًا اَنْ يَكْبَرُوا
وَمَنْ كَانَ غَنِيًّا فَلْيَسْتَعْفِفْ وَمَنْ كَانَ فَقِيرًا فَلْيَاْكُلْ
بِالْمَعْرُوفِ فَاِذَا دَفَعْتُمْ اِلَيْهِمْ اَمْوَالَهُمْ فَاَشْهِدُوا عَلَيْهِمْ وَكَفَى
بِاللهِ حَسِيبًا ۞ وَلْيَخْشَ الَّذِينَ لَوْ تَرَكُوا مِنْ خَلْفِهِمْ ذُرِّيَّةً
ضِعَافًا خَافُوا عَلَيْهِمْ فَلْيَتَّقُوا اللهَ وَلْيَقُولُوا قَوْلًا سَدِيدًا ۞ اِنَّ
الَّذِينَ يَاْكُلُونَ اَمْوَالَ الْيَتَامَى ظُلْمًا اِنَّمَا يَاْكُلُونَ فِى بُطُونِهِمْ
نَارًا وَسَيَصْلَوْنَ سَعِيرًا ۞

"And make not over your property, which Allāh
has made a (means of) support for you, to the
weak of understanding,[1] and maintain them

---

1. Minors or orphans, who have not sufficient prudence for the management of their affairs (see next note).

out of it, and clothe them and give them a good
education. And test the orphans until they
reach the age of marriage. Then if you find in
them maturity of intellect,[1] make over to them
their property, and consume it not extravagantly
and hastily against their growing up. And
whoever is rich, let him abstain, and whoever is
poor let him consume reasonably.[2] And when
you make over to them their property, call
witnesses in their presence. And Allāh is enough
as a Reckoner . . . And let those fear who,
should they leave behind them weakly offspring
would fear on their account; so let them
observe their duty to Allāh, and let them
‚speak right words. Those who swallow the
property of the orphans unjustly, they do but
swallow fire into their bellies. And they
will burn in blazing fire" — 4 : 5-6; 9-10.

This, which God has taught, is true honesty
and faithfulness, and its various requisites are
clearly set forth in the verses quoted above.
Honesty which lacks any of these requisites cannot
be classed as one of the high morals but a natural

---

1. For which the proper limit is eighteen, and where you perceive that
they are able to manage their affairs well. However, if maturity of
intellect is not attained at this age, the limit may be extended. These
words, moreover, show that marriage should be performed when a person
has attained majority, for the age of marriage is spoken as being the age
of attaining majority.

2. Note that it was a well-known rule among the Arabs that the guardians
of an orphan's property, if they had a mind to take any remuneration for
their services, took it, so long as possible, out of the profit which the trade
brought in and did not touch the capital. The Quran permits the taking
of recompense in this reasonable manner.

condition in its crude stage and not proof against every breach of faith. Elsewhere, we are told:

اِنَّ اللهَ لَا يُحِبُّ الْخَائِنِينَ ۞

"Surely Allāh loves not the treacherous" — 8 : 58.

اِنَّ اللهَ يَأْمُرُكُمْ اَنْ تُؤَدُّوا الْاَمٰنٰتِ اِلٰۤى اَهْلِهَا

"Surely Allāh commands you to make over trusts to those worthy of them . . ." — 4 : 58.

وَلَا تَأْكُلُوا اَمْوَالَكُمْ بَيْنَكُمْ بِالْبَاطِلِ
وَتُدْلُوا بِهَا اِلَى الْحُكَّامِ لِتَأْكُلُوا فَرِيْقًا مِّنْ
اَمْوَالِ النَّاسِ بِالْاِثْمِ وَاَنْتُمْ تَعْلَمُوْنَ

"And swallow not up your property among yourselves by false means, nor seek to gain access thereby to the judges, so that you may swallow up a part of the property of men wrongfully while you know" — 2 : 188.

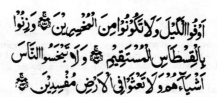

"Give full measure and be not of those who diminish. And weigh with a true balance. And

wrong not men of their dues, and act not corruptly
in the earth, making mischief "[1] — 26: 181-183.

وَلَا تَتَبَدَّلُوا الْخَبِيثَ بِالطَّيِّبِ

"(O people) and do not substitute worthless
(things) for (their) good (ones) . . . "[2]— 4 : 2.

These are comprehensive injunctions against
all sorts of dishonest dealings, and every breach
of faith comes within them. Separate offences
are not enumerated here, as a comprehensive
list of them would have required much space.
The Holy Book has, therefore, made a general
statement which comprehends in its plain meaning
all sorts of dishonesty. In short, a person who
shows honesty in some of his dealings, but is not
scrupulous about it to the minutest degree and does
not observe all good rules, is not gifted with the
moral quality but acts out of habit in obedience
to the natural inclination and without applying
the faculty of reason.

Meekness

Coming to the third stage of morals falling
within the first division, we have to deal with the
quality known in Arabic as *hudna* (or *hūn*) or

---

1. That is, committing theft or dacoity, or picking pockets, or otherwise
unlawfully seizing other man's property.
2. For, as it is unlawful for one person to lay hold of another's substance
wrongfully, so is it also unjust to sell thing of an inferior quality.

meekness". It consists in refraining from causing
bodily injury to another person and thus leading
a peaceful life upon earth. Peaceableness is, no
doubt, a blessing for humanity and must be valued
for the great good which proceeds from it.

The natural inclination, out of which this
moral quality develops, is witnessed in a child in
the form of attachment. It is plain that, divested
of reason, man can neither realize peaceableness
nor hostility. A natural inclination towards
submission and attachment so early witnessed in
the child is, therefore, only the germ out of which
grows the high moral quality of peaceableness.
It cannot itself be classed as moral as long as it is
not consciously resorted to on the recommendation
of reason. It is otherwise when reason and judge-
ment come to its assistance. The directions
contained in the Quran may be briefly quoted:

وَعِبَادُ الرَّحْمٰنِ الَّذِينَ يَمْشُونَ عَلَى الْأَرْضِ هَوْنًا

"And the servants of the Beneficent are they
who walk on the earth in humility . . ." — 25: 63.

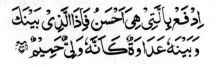

"Repel (evil) with what is best, when lo! he

between whom and thee is enmity would
be as if he were a warm friend" — 41 : 34.

$$وَالصُّلْحُ خَيْرٌ$$

"And reconciliation is better . . ." — 4: 128.

$$وَأَصْلِحُوا ذَاتَ بَيْنِكُمْ$$

"And set aright your differences . . ." — 8 : 1.

$$وَإِنْ جَنَحُوا لِلسَّلْمِ فَاجْنَحْ لَهَا$$

"And if they (the enemy) incline to peace,
incline thou also to it . . . " — 8 : 61.

$$وَ الَّذِينَ لَا يَشْهَدُونَ الزُّورَ وَإِذَا مَرُّوا بِاللَّغْوِ مَرُّوا كِرَامًا$$

"They who witness no falsehood, and when they
pass by what is vain they pass by nobly"[1]— 25:72.

This verse means that the believers should
not take up an hostile attitude so long as no
material injury is caused to them. The guiding
principle of peaceableness is that one should not be
offended at the slightest opposition to one's feelings.

---

1. The word *laghw*, used in this verse, needs to be explained. A word or
deed is said to be *laghw* (frivolous) when it causes no substantial loss or
material injury to its object, although done or said with a mischievous or
bad intention. Meekness requires that no notice should be taken of such
words or deeds and that a man should behave like a gentleman on such
occasions. But if the injury is not trivial and causes material loss to life,
property or honour, the quality required to meet such an emergency is not
meekness but forgiveness, which will be discussed in the following pages.

Politeness

The fourth and last of the morals of the first division is *rifq* or "politeness". The preliminary stage of this quality, as witnessed in the child, is *talāqat* or "cheerfulness". Before the child learns to speak, the cheerfulness of its face serves the same purpose as kind words in a grown-up man. But the propriety of the occasion is an essential condition in classing politeness as a high moral quality:

لَا يَسْخَرْ قَوْمٌ مِنْ قَوْمٍ عَسَىٰٓ أَنْ يَكُونُوا خَيْرًا مِّنْهُمْ وَ لَا نِسَاءٌ مِّنْ نِّسَاءٍ عَسَىٰٓ أَنْ يَكُنَّ خَيْرًا مِّنْهُنَّ وَ لَا تَلْمِزُوٓا أَنْفُسَكُمْ وَ لَا تَنَابَزُوا بِالْأَلْقَابِ بِئْسَ الِاسْمُ الْفُسُوقُ بَعْدَ الْإِيمَانِ وَ مَنْ لَّمْ يَتُبْ فَأُولَٰٓئِكَ هُمُ الظَّالِمُونَ ۞ يَٰٓأَيُّهَا الَّذِينَ آمَنُوا اجْتَنِبُوا كَثِيرًا مِّنَ الظَّنِّ إِنَّ بَعْضَ الظَّنِّ إِثْمٌ وَّ لَا تَجَسَّسُوا وَ لَا يَغْتَبْ بَّعْضُكُمْ بَعْضًا أَيُحِبُّ أَحَدُكُمْ أَنْ يَّأْكُلَ لَحْمَ أَخِيهِ مَيْتًا فَكَرِهْتُمُوهُ وَ اتَّقُوا اللهَ إِنَّ اللهَ تَوَّابٌ رَّحِيمٌ ۞

"(O you who believe) let not people laugh at people, perchance they may be better than they; nor let women (laugh) at women, perchance they may be better than they. Neither find fault with your own people, nor call one another by nick-names. Evil is a bad name after faith;

and whoso turns not, these it is that are the iniquitous. O you who believe, avoid most of suspicion, for surely suspicion in some cases is sin; and spy not nor let some of you backbite others. Does one of you like to eat the flesh of his dead brother? You abhor it! And keep your duty to Allāh, surely Allāh is Oft-returning (to mercy), Merciful" — 49: 11-12.

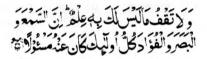

"And speak good (words) to (all) men" — 2:83.

"(O man) and follow not that of which thou hast no knowledge. Surely the hearing and the sight and the heart — of each of these it will (surely) be asked" — 17 : 36.

Such are the wonderful teachings of the Holy Book on the subject of politeness!

Forgiveness

Having dealt with the first division of morals — those relating to the avoidance of mischief — we now come to the second heading under which we shall give examples of the moral qualities taught by the Quran for doing good to others. The first of these is *'afw* or "forgiveness". The person to

whom a real injury has been caused has the right
to redress by bringing the offender to law or
himself dealing out suitable punishment to him;
and when he foregoes his right and forgives the
offender, he does him a real good. Thus we read:

وَالْكَاظِمِينَ الْغَيْظَ وَالْعَافِينَ عَنِ النَّاسِ

"And those who restrain (their) anger and
are forgiving toward mankind ... " — 3 : 133.

وَجَزَاؤُا سَيِّئَةٍ سَيِّئَةٌ مِثْلُهَا فَمَنْ عَفَا وَأَصْلَحَ فَأَجْرُهُ عَلَى اللهِ

"And the recompense of evil is punishment
like it; but whoever forgives and amends,
his reward is with Allāh ... " — 42 : 40.

It will be noted that these verses furnish the
guiding rule as to the occasions of forgiveness. The
Quran does not teach unconditional forgiveness
and non-resistance of evil on every occasion, nor
does it inculcate that punishment is not to be given
to the offender under any circumstances. The
principle which it lays down commends itself to
every reasonable person. It requires the injured
person to exercise his judgment, and see whether
the occasion calls for punishment or forgiveness.
The course which is calculated to improve matters
should then be adopted. The offender would,
under certain circumstances, benefit by forgiveness
and mend his ways for the future. But on other
occasions forgiveness may produce the contrary

effect and embolden the culprit to do worse deeds. The Word of God does not, therefore, enjoin nor even permit that we should go on forgiving faults blindly. It requires us to consider what course is likely to lead to real good. As there are people of vindictive nature, who carry the spirit of revenge to an excess and do not forget an injury for generations, there are others who are ready to yield and prone to forgive on every occasion.

Excess in mildness, like excess in vengeance, leads to dangerous consequences. The person who winks at gross immoralities or forbears an attack upon his honour or chastity may be said to forgive, but his forgiveness is a weakness that strikes at the root of nobility, chastity and self-respect. No sensible person could praise it as a high moral quality. It is for this reason that the Quran places the limits of propriety even upon forgiveness and does not recognize every display of this quality as a moral quality unless it is shown upon the right occasion. The mere giving up of a claim to requital from an offender, whatever the circumstances and however serious the nature of the offence, is far from being a great moral quality to which men should aspire.

The mere presence of this quality in a person, therefore, does not entitle him to any credit unless he shows us, by its use on the right occasion, that he possesses it as a moral quality. The distinction between natural and moral qualities should be clearly remembered. The innate or natural qualities are transformed into moral qualities when a person refrains from doing an act upon the right occasion and after due consideration of the good or evil that is likely to result from it. Many of the lower animals are quite harmless and do not resist when evil is done to them. A cow may be said to be innocent, and a lamb meek, but to neither do we attribute the high moral qualities which man aspires after, for they are not gifted with reason. It is the occasion only upon which anything is done that justifies or condemns a deed, and the Word of God has, therefore, imposed this condition upon every moral quality.

Kindness

The second moral quality by means of which man can do good (to others) is ʿadal or "good for good"; the third is iḥsān or "kindness", and the fourth ʿitāi dhiʾl-qurbā or "kindness to kindred" :

"Surely Allāh enjoins justice and the doing of good (to others), and the giving to the kindred, and He forbids indecency and abomination and wickedness . . ." — 16: 90.

This verse calls attention to three stages in the doing of good. The lowest stage is that in which man does good to his benefactors only. Even an ordinary man who has the sense to appreciate the goodness of others can acquire this quality and do good in return for good. From this, there is an advancement to the second stage in which a man takes the initiative to do good to others. It consists in bestowing favours upon persons who cannot claim them as a right. This quality, excellent as it is, occupies a middle position. To it often attaches the infirmity that the doer expects thanks or prayers in return for the good he does, and the slightest opposition from the object of compassion is likely to be felt as ungratefulness. He would fain have an acknowledgement of the benefit conferred and is led sometimes to take advantage of his position by laying upon the other some burden which he would not have otherwise willingly borne. In order to remedy this, the Holy Book has warned the doer of good thus :

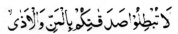

"(O you who believe) make not your charity worthless by reproach and injury. . ."[1] — 2 : 264.

---

1. In this verse, the word *ṣadaqa* (charity) is derived from *ṣidq* (sincerity). If, therefore, there is no sincerity in the deed, alms are of no effect, being mere show. In other words, this is an infirmity attached to the doing of good to another that the doer is led sometimes to remind the person relieved of his obligation or to boast of it.

A third stage has, therefore, been pointed out by the Word of God. To attain this perfection, man should not think of the good he has done nor expect even an expression of thankfulness from the person upon whom the benefit has been conferred. The good should proceed from sincere sympathy like that which is shown by the nearest relatives — by a mother, for instance, for her children. This is the last and the highest stage of kindness to the creatures of God and, beyond this, man cannot aspire to anything higher. This stage has been termed "kindness to kindred". But from the lowest to the highest form of doing good, an essential condition has been imposed upon all: that it should be done on the proper occasion; for the verse affirms that these noble qualities are liable, unless exercised with great care, to degenerate into vices. *'Adl* (good for good) becomes *fahshā* — an undue excess productive of harm rather than good; *ihsān* (kindness) becomes *munkar* — a thing which, when ill-bestowed, conscience rejects and from which reason recoils; *'itāi dhi 'l-qurbā* (kindness to kindred), when directed to a wrong end, becomes *baghī* — the rain which, by its excess, destroys the crops. Therefore, any excess or deficiency in the doing of that which would otherwise have been most beneficial is termed "oppression". Nor is the mere doing of good in any of the three forms above-mentioned

a high moral quality unless attested to as such
by the propriety of the occasion and the exercise
of judgment. These are natural conditions and
inborn qualities which are transformed into moral
qualities by good judgment and by their display
on the right occasion.

Upon the subject of *iḥsān* (kindness), the Holy
Book has also the following injunctions:

أَحْسِنُوا ۛ إِنَّ اللَّهَ يُحِبُّ الْمُحْسِنِينَ

"(Spend in Allāh's way) and do good (to others).
Surely Allāh loves the doers of good" — 2: 195.

يَا أَيُّهَا الَّذِينَ آمَنُوا أَنْفِقُوا مِنْ طَيِّبَاتِ مَا كَسَبْتُمْ
وَمِمَّا أَخْرَجْنَا لَكُمْ مِنَ الْأَرْضِ وَلَا تَيَمَّمُوا الْخَبِيثَ

"O you who believe, spend of the good things
that you earn and of that which We bring
forth for you out of the earth, and aim not
at the bad to spend thereof . . ."[1] — 2: 267.

إِنَّ الْأَبْرَارَ يَشْرَبُونَ مِنْ كَأْسٍ كَانَ مِزَاجُهَا كَافُورًا
عَيْنًا يَشْرَبُ بِهَا عِبَادُ اللَّهِ يُفَجِّرُونَهَا تَفْجِيرًا

"The righteous shall truly drink of a cup
tempered with camphor — a fountain from

---

1. That is, in which there is no mixture of property acquired by
theft or bribe, or misappropriation, or by oppression, or by any other
dishonest or unjust means.

which the (faithful) servants of Allāh drink,
making it flow in abundance"[1] — 76 : 5-6.

وَالَّذِينَ إِذَآ أَنْفَقُوا لَمْ يُسْرِفُوا وَلَمْ يَقْتُرُوا
وَكَانَ بَيْنَ ذَٰلِكَ قَوَامًا ۝

"And they who, when they spend, are neither
extravagant nor parsimonious, and the just
mean is ever between the two" — 25 : 67

وَيُطْعِمُونَ الطَّعَامَ عَلَىٰ حُبِّهِ مِسْكِينًا وَيَتِيمًا وَأَسِيرًا ۝ إِنَّمَا
نُطْعِمُكُمْ لِوَجْهِ اللَّهِ لَا نُرِيدُ مِنْكُمْ جَزَآءً وَّلَا شُكُورًا ۝

"And they give food, out of love for Him, to the
poor and the orphan and the captive. We feed
you, for Allāh's pleasure only — We desire from
you neither reward nor thanks"[2] — 76 : 8-9.

وَآتَى الْمَالَ عَلَىٰ حُبِّهِ ذَوِي الْقُرْبَىٰ وَالْيَتَمَىٰ وَالْمَسَاكِينَ
وَابْنَ السَّبِيلِ وَالسَّآئِلِينَ وَفِي الرِّقَابِ

"And (the righteous is he who) gives away wealth
out of love for Him to the near of kin and the

---

1. In this verse, the word *kāfūr* (camphor) is derived from *kafr* (to suppress;
to cover) and, therefore, by the quaffing of camphor drink is here meant
that the unlawful passions of the righteous shall be suppressed, that their
hearts shall be cleaned of every impurity, and that they shall be refrigerated
with the coolness of the knowledge of God.　The verse goes on to say:
"The servants of God (*i.e.*, those who do good) shall drink on the Day of
Judgment of a spring which they are making to gush forth with their own
hands".　This verse throws light upon the secret which underlies the
true philosophy of Paradise.

2.　This verse recommends the third stage of doing good, which proceeds
out of sincere sympathy and seeks no reward, not even an acknowledgement
of the obligation conferred.

orphans and the needy and the wayfarer and to
those who ask and to set slaves free. . ."—2:177.

وَأَنْفَقُوا مِمَّا رَزَقْنَاهُمْ سِرًّا وَعَلَانِيَةً

"And (those who) spend of that which We have
given them, secretly and openly. . . "—13:22.

الَّذِينَ يُنْفِقُونَ فِي السَّرَّآءِ وَالضَّرَّآءِ

"Those who spend (of that which Allāh has given
them) in ease and in adversity . . . " — 3 : 133.

وَفِي أَمْوَالِهِمْ حَقٌّ لِلسَّآئِلِ وَالْمَحْرُومِ

"In their (those who keep from evil) wealth
there was a due share for the beggar and
for one who is denied (good)"[1] — 51 : 19.

إِنَّمَا الصَّدَقَاتُ لِلْفُقَرَآءِ وَالْمَسَاكِينِ وَالْعَامِلِينَ عَلَيْهَا
وَالْمُؤَلَّفَةِ قُلُوبُهُمْ وَفِي الرِّقَابِ وَالْغَارِمِينَ وَفِي سَبِيلِ
اللَّهِ وَابْنِ السَّبِيلِ فَرِيضَةً مِنَ اللَّهِ

"Charity (zakāt) is only for the poor and the
needy, and those employed to administer it, and
those whose hearts are made to incline (to truth),
and (to free) the captives, and those in debt,

---

1. It is to be noted that the poor are here spoken of as having a share in
the wealth of the rich. The State is bound to take that share and make
it over to the poor. But it is only a share, not the whole — Publisher.

and in the way of Allāh and for the wayfarer — an ordinance from Allāh . . . "[1]— 9 : 60.

لَنْ تَنَالُوا الْبِرَّ حَتَّى تُنْفِقُوا مِمَّا تُحِبُّونَ

"You cannot attain to righteousness unless you
spend out of what you love . . . " — 3 : 91.

وَآتِ ذَا الْقُرْبَى حَقَّهُ وَالْمِسْكِينَ وَ ابْنَ
السَّبِيلِ وَلَا تُبَذِّرْ تَبْذِيرًا

"And give to the near of kin his due
and (to) the needy, and the wayfarer, and
squander not (thy) wealth wastefully" — 17 : 26.

وَبِالْوَالِدَيْنِ إِحْسَانًا وَبِذِى الْقُرْبَى وَالْيَتَامَى وَالْمَسَاكِينِ
وَالْجَارِ ذِى الْقُرْبَى وَالْجَارِ الْجُنُبِ وَالصَّاحِبِ بِالْجَنْبِ وَابْنِ
السَّبِيلِ وَمَا مَلَكَتْ أَيْمَانُكُمْ إِنَّ اللهَ لَا يُحِبُّ مَنْ كَانَ
مُخْتَالًا فَخُورًا الَّذِينَ يَبْخَلُونَ وَيَأْمُرُونَ النَّاسَ
بِالْبُخْلِ وَيَكْتُمُونَ مَا آتَاهُمُ اللهُ مِنْ فَضْلِهِ

"And be good to the parents and to the near of
kin and the orphans and the needy and the
neighbour of (your) kin and the alien neighbour,

---

1. That by *ṣadaqāt* here is meant the obligatory charity, called *zakāt*,
and not voluntary alms, is shown by the concluding words of the verse,
which call it an ordinance from Allāh — Publisher.

and the companion in a journey and the wayfarer and those whom your right hands possess.
Surely Allāh loves not such as are proud, boast-
ful, who are niggardly and bid people to be
niggardly and hide that which Allāh has
given them out of His Grace . . ." — 4 : 36-37.

It may be noted that "those whom your
right hands possess" may be your servants or even
your domestic animals.

Courage

The fifth virtue, which resembles the instinct
of bravery, is *shajā'at* or "courage". A child,
when it has no reason, displays bravery and is
ready to thrust its hands into the fire because,
having no knowledge of the consequences, the
instinctive quality is predominant in it. Man,
in a similar condition, fearlessly rushes forth even
to fight lions and other wild beasts, and stands
out alone in the hour of contest against all armies.
People would think that this is the highest courage
but the fact is that it is more a mechanical movement than a moral quality. Wild beasts are on an
equality with him at this level. The virtue which
we call "courage" can be displayed only after
due reasoning and reflection and after full consideration of the propriety or the impropriety of the
act. It is a quality which can be classed as an
exalted virtue only when displayed on the right

occasion. The Holy Book contains the following directions upon this point:

وَالَّذِينَ صَبَرُوا ابْتِغَاءَ وَجْهِ رَبِّهِمْ

"And those who are steadfast[1] in seeking the countenance of their Lord . . . " — 13 : 22.

الَّذِينَ قَالَ لَهُمُ النَّاسُ إِنَّ النَّاسَ قَدْ
جَمَعُوا لَكُمْ فَاخْشَوْهُمْ فَزَادَهُمْ إِيمَانًا
وَقَالُوا حَسْبُنَا اللَّهُ وَنِعْمَ الْوَكِيلُ

"Those to whom men said: Surely the people have gathered against you, so fear them; but this (threat) increased their faith, and they said: Allāh is sufficient for us and He is the most excellent Guardian"[2] — 3 : 172.

وَالصَّابِرِينَ فِي الْبَأْسَاءِ وَالضَّرَّاءِ
وَحِينَ الْبَأْسِ أُولَٰئِكَ الَّذِينَ صَدَقُوا

"And the patient in distress and affliction and in the time of conflict. These are they who are

---

1. Patience in trials is only one of the ideas which *ṣabr* conveys.
2. The courage of these people is not like the bravery of wild beasts, a mechanical movement depending upon passions and therefore flowing in one direction only; they utilize their courage in two ways: through it they resist and overcome the passions of the flesh and again resist the attacks of an evil-doer when it is advisable to do so, not in obedience to brute force but in the cause of truth. They do not, moreover, trust their own selves, but have their confidence in the support of God at the time of trials.

truthful. (Such are God-fearing) " — 2 : 177.

وَ لَا تَكُونُوۡا كَالَّذِیۡنَ خَرَجُوۡا مِنۡ دِیَارِهِمۡ بَطَرًا وَّرِئَآءَ النَّاسِ

"And be not like those who came forth from their homes exultingly and to be seen of men"—8: 47.

The truly courageous do not display their bravery in an insolent manner. Their only consideration is the pleasure of God. All this leads to the conclusion that true courage takes its root in patience and steadfastness. The courageous person resists his passion and does not fly from danger like a coward but, before he takes any step, he looks to the remote consequences of his action. Between the daring dash of a savage and the indomitable courage of a civilized man there is this vast difference that the latter is prepared to meet real dangers but he reasons and reflects, even in the fury of battle, before he proceeds and takes the course best-suited to avert the evil, while the former — in obedience to an irresistible passion — makes a violent onset in one direction only.

Veracity

The sixth virtue, which is developed out of the natural conditions, is *ṣidq* or "veracity". So long as there is no incentive to tell a lie, man is naturally inclined to speak the truth. He is averse to lying from his very nature and hates the person who is proved to have told a lie. But this

natural condition cannot claim our respect as one
of the noble moral qualities. Unless a man is
purged of the low motives which bar him from
truth, his veracity is questionable. For, if he
speaks the truth only in matters in which truth
does no harm to himself and tells a lie or holds his
tongue from the utterance of truth when his life
or property or honour is at stake, he can claim no
superiority over children and madmen. In fact, no
one tells a lie without a motive, and there is no
virtue in resorting to truth so long as there is no
apprehension of harm. The test of truth is the
occasion when one's life or honour or property is
in danger. The Quran contains the following:

وَإِذَا قُلْتُمْ فَاعْدِلُوا وَلَوْ كَانَ ذَا قُرْبَى

"And when you speak, be just, even though
it be (against) a relative . . . " — 6 : 153.

وَلَا تَكْتُمُوا الشَّهَادَةَ وَمَنْ يَكْتُمْهَا فَإِنَّهُ آثِمٌ قَلْبُهُ

"And conceal not testimony. And whoever conceals it, his heart is surely sinful" — 2 : 283.

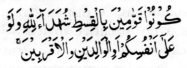

"(O you who believe) be maintainers of
justice, bearers of witness for Allāh, even

though it be against your own selves or (your)
parents or near relatives . . . " — 4 : 135.

أَعَدَّ اللَّهُ لَهُم مَّغْفِرَةً وَأَجْرًا عَظِيمًا

"(And the truthful men and the truthful
women . . .) Allāh has prepared for them
forgiveness and a mighty reward" — 33 : 35.

وَتَوَاصَوْا بِالْحَقِّ وَتَوَاصَوْا بِالصَّبْرِ

"And (those who) exhort one another to Truth,
and exhort one another to patience" — 103 : 3.

وَلَا يَجْرِمَنَّكُمْ شَنَآنُ قَوْمٍ عَلَىٰ أَلَّا تَعْدِلُوا

"(O you who believe) let not hatred of a people
incite you not to act equitably . . . " — 5 : 8.

وَالَّذِينَ لَا يَشْهَدُونَ الزُّورَ وَإِذَا مَرُّوا بِاللَّغْوِ مَرُّوا كِرَامًا

"And they who will witness no falsehood,
and when they pass by what is vain, they
(indeed) pass by with dignity" — 25 : 72.

فَاجْتَنِبُوا الرِّجْسَ مِنَ الْأَوْثَانِ وَاجْتَنِبُوا قَوْلَ الزُّورِ

"(O you who believe) shun the filth of the
idols, and shun false words" — 22 : 30.

It may be recalled that shunning of idols
and falsehood is enjoined in the same breath to
indicate that falsehood is an idol, and the person
who trusts in it does not trust in the Almighty.

Patience

Another virtue, which develops out of the natural conditions of man, is *ṣabr* or "patience". Everyone has more or less to suffer misfortunes, diseases and afflictions which are the common lot of humanity. Everyone has also, after much sorrowing and suffering, to make his peace with the misfortunes that befall him. But such contentment is by no means a noble moral quality.

It is a natural consequence of the continuance of affliction that weariness at last brings about conciliation. The first shock causes depression of spirits and inquietude and elicits wails of woe, but when the excitement of the moment is over, there is necessarily a reaction for the extreme has been reached. But such disappointment and contentment are both the result of natural inclinations. It is only when the loss is received with total resignation to the will of God that the sufferer deserves to be called virtuous:

وَلَنَبْلُوَنَّكُمْ بِشَيْءٍ مِّنَ الْخَوْفِ وَالْجُوعِ وَنَقْصٍ مِّنَ الْأَمْوَالِ
وَالْأَنْفُسِ وَالثَّمَرَاتِ وَبَشِّرِ الصَّابِرِينَ ۞ الَّذِينَ إِذَا أَصَابَتْهُمْ
مُصِيبَةٌ قَالُوا إِنَّا لِلَّهِ وَإِنَّا إِلَيْهِ رَاجِعُونَ ۞ أُولَٰئِكَ عَلَيْهِمْ
صَلَوَاتٌ مِّن رَّبِّهِمْ وَرَحْمَةٌ ۚ وَأُولَٰئِكَ هُمُ الْمُهْتَدُونَ ۞

"And We shall certainly try you with something of fear and hunger and loss of property and lives

and fruits. And give good news to the patient,
who, when a misfortune befalls them, say :
'Surely we are Allāh's, and to Him we shall
return'. Those are they on whom are blessings
and mercy from their Lord ; and those are the
followers of the right course" — 2 : 155-157.

It is, therefore, owing to the quality of patience
that a man declares himself satisfied with God's
pleasure. In another sense it is also justice; for
when the Lord has made numerous provisions in
accordance with the pleasure of man and does,
on so many occasions in his life, bring about
things as he desires, and has provided him with
numerous blessings, it would be highly unjust if a
man should grumble because the Creator wills a
thing in another way and should not take the
good that He provides with cheerfulness but turn
aside from His path.

Sympathy

Another quality falling under the same category
is *muwāsāt* or "sympathy". People of every natio-
nality and religion are naturally endowed with
the feeling of sympathy and, in their zeal for
the interests of their countrymen or co-religionists,
throw scruples to the wind, and do not hesitate to
wrong others. Such sympathetic zeal, however,
does not proceed out of moral feelings but is an
instinctive passion, and is witnessed even in the

lower animals, especially ravens in whose case
the call of one brings together thousands of them.
To be classed as a moral quality, it must be displayed in accordance with the principles of justice
and equity, and on the proper occasion:

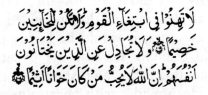

وَتَعَاوَنُوا عَلَى الْبِرِّ وَالتَّقْوَى وَلَا تَعَاوَنُوا عَلَى الْإِثْمِ وَالْعُدْوَانِ

"(O you who believe) help one another in
righteousness and piety and help not one another in sin and aggression . . . " — 5 : 2.

لَا تَهِنُوا فِي ابْتِغَاءِ الْقَوْمِ وَلَا هَكَّنَ لِلْخَائِنِينَ
خَصِيمًا وَلَا تُجَادِلْ عَنِ الَّذِينَ يَخْتَانُونَ
أَنْفُسَهُمْ إِنَّ اللهَ لَا يُحِبُّ مَنْ كَانَ خَوَّانًا أَثِيمًا

"And be not weak-hearted in pursuit of the
enemy . . . And be not one pleading the
case of the dishonest . . . And contend not
on behalf of those who act unfaithfully to
their souls. Surely Allāh loves not him
who is treacherous, sinful" — 4 : 104-107.

Existence of God

Of the innate feeling of man, which we see
implanted in his very nature, is a search after an
Almighty Being to Whom he is drawn by a hidden
magnetic power acting upon his soul. Its first
manifestation takes place with the birth of the
child. As soon as the child is born, it is led by a

desire to incline to its mother and, corresponding to the material instinct of love, it shows an instinctive impulse of attachment to its mother. With its growth and the development of its faculties, this instinct is displayed more prominently. It finds no rest but in the lap of its mother, and no peace but in her tender caresses. Separation from her embitters all its pleasures, and no blessing, however great, can atone for the pain caused to it by her loss. It has no consciousness, but is impelled by instinct to love its mother, and finds no repose but in her bosom.

The attraction, which thus draws the child towards its parents, points to the secret magnetism implanted by nature in the soul of man which draws him to his Creator. It is this same attraction again which excites the affections of man to tend towards, and take their rest in, some external object. Thus we find the principle of attraction towards God deeply implanted within us and instinctively impressed upon our hearts. The emotions of love, however different the objects which call them forth, are all to be traced to the instinct of love for the Benefactor. In fixing his affections upon other objects, man seems only to be searching for the real object. He has, as it were, lost something of which he has now forgotten the name, and seems to be seeking it under every other object that he comes across. The attraction of wealth, the charm of beauty and the fascination of sweet and enchanting voices are only so many indications of some greater power underlying all these which draws all hearts towards it.

But, as imperfect human reason cannot comprehend nor the material eye discover this mysterious Being Who, hidden like heat in the soul, is invisible to all, the true knowledge of His existence has been attended with the greatest difficulties, and mistakes have been made in connection with His recognition. Superstition and gross credulity have accorded the homage due to the Invisible God to frail creatures and material objects. This has been well illustrated by the Quran in a simile where the world is likened to a crystal palace paved with bright glass. Under this transparent floor, a strong current of water is flowing. A superficial eye that witnesses the scene mistakes the glass for the water, being unable to discover the truth. That through which the water is seen, is wrongly taken as water itself:

قِيلَ لَهَا ادْخُلِى الصَّرْحَ ۖ فَلَمَّا رَأَتْهُ حَسِبَتْهُ لُجَّةً وَّ
كَشَفَتْ عَنْ سَاقَيْهَا ۚ قَالَ اِنَّهُ صَرْحٌ مُّمَرَّدٌ مِّنْ قَوَارِيرَ ۗ

"It was said to her (the queen of Sheba): Enter the palace. But when she saw it she deemed it to be a great expanse of water, and prepared herself to meet the difficulty. He (Solomon) said: Surely it is a palace made smooth with glass..." — 27 : 44.

Same is the case with great heavenly bodies which are seen in the universe, such as the sun, the moon and the stars, which only reveal the existence of the Powerful Being, working behind them all. But faulty human judgment makes a person bow in worship before them under the same delusion as the eye in the above instance mistook transparent glass for water. The Being that manifests Himself through these bodies is quite different from the bodies themselves. The polytheist is unwise enough to attribute the work done by the great Power to the material objects through which that power is manifested.

In short, although God reveals Himself manifestly, He is invisible and hidden. The material universe cannot lead us to an undeniable conclusion — to absolute certainty regarding the existence of its Author. The consummate order and perfect arrangement which the material eye discovers in the universe, comprising countless heavenly bodies and numerous wonders which are disclosed to a thinking mind in nature, have never led, and can never lead, to the firm conviction, to the perfect certainty that there truly exists a God, the Creator and the Lord of the worlds.

The greatest astronomers and philosophers, who have applied their minds and energies solely to those sciences, have been involved in fatal doubts and scepticism as to the existence of God. All their knowledge, if it ever led them to draw the conclusion of the existence of the Almighty, could never go further than set it down among the probabilities. The creation of the sun, the moon and the stars, the order and design witnessed in those orbs which constitute the host of heaven, the consummate laws of order that regulate the universe, the formation of man's body and mind, the marvellous power and wisdom discernible in the government of this universe, no doubt, lead all to the conclusion of the probability of the existence of a Creator, but probability does not prove actual existence.

There is a vast difference between a probability and a certainty. Unless there is firm persuasion and strong conviction that God actually exists, the darkness of doubt cannot be dispelled and true light can never enter the heart. The rational persuasion, following from observation of a plan in the universe, does not amount to a certainty and cannot lead to peace and contentment of mind. It is not the wholesome cup of elixir which has the power to wash off every doubt and quench the thirst which the soul of man naturally feels for a true and perfect knowledge of the Lord. The imperfect knowledge, which is the result of a study of nature, is fraught with danger, for there is in it more of argument than substantial reality.

Unless the Almighty reveals Himself by His word spoken to His servants, as He reveals Himself by His works as witnessed in nature, a rational persuasion of His existence, which is the outcome of an observation of His work, is never satisfactory. If, for instance, the doors of a room are all latched from inside, the natural inference would be that there is someone in the room who has bolted the doors. But if years pass by and no sound is heard from within, no voice responds to the repeated calls of the outsider for years, we would have to change our opinion as to the presence of someone within and would ascribe the event to some incomprehensible circumstance. Such is the belief in the existence of God, based upon a study of nature; the whole inquiry brings us but to the conclusion that chances are in favour of the existence of a Creator.

The fact is that an inquiry relating to the existence of God cannot be complete so long as we consider only one side of the question: the work of the Lord. The effort is misdirected which sets before itself the object of discovering the Creator simply from under heaps of matter. It is a blasphemy against the glorious and living Benefactor that, in the midst of all His creation, He should be likened to a dead body which can only be discovered by digging it out from under heaps of dust. That God, with all His infinite wisdom and almighty power, should depend upon human effort to be revealed to the world, is a shocking idea. The Supreme Being, viewed in this light, can never be the centre of our hopes and our Supporter in all our infirmities. Does the Creator Himself reveal His face to His creatures, or are they to seek a clue to His existence for themselves? Does He show us His presence, or are we to search for Him? The external and invisible God has eternally made Himself known by His own clear and blessed voice proclaiming "I am", and has thus invited His frail creatures towards Himself that they may seek their support in Him.

It is presumptuous to assert that the Almighty lies under an obligation to man, because the latter takes the trouble to discover Him and that, but for man's exertions, the Eternal and Immortal Lord of the Universe would never have been known to His creation. To object to the palpable and conclusive proof of the real existence of God as furnished by His voice on the ground that He must have a tongue — an idea inconsistent with the concept of God as a Spirit — is baseless. Has He not created the earth and the host of heaven without any material hands? Does He not see the whole world without any material eyes? Does He not hear the voice of His servants and yet has no ear like ours? Is it not necessary, then, that He should speak as He creates, sees and hears? To object to one attribute while admitting others is quite illogical.

To say that though the Divine Being spoke to generations of men in the past and made Himself known to them by His clear voice, yet He does not speak now, would be to assert something wholly untenable. The unchangeable Lord, Who spoke in the past, speaks even now, and blesses with His holy word such of His servants as seek Him with all their heart and soul. His chosen ones even now drink deep at the fountain of His inspiration; no one ever set a seal upon His lips. His grace even now flows in abundance and is bestowed upon men as it was bestowed of old.

It is true that revelation of a perfect law and necessary rules for the guidance of mankind has put an end to the need of a fresh revealed law, and apostleship and prophecy have attained perfection in the holy person of Prophet Muḥammad, but access to the sacred fountain of inspiration is not thereby barred.

That the Divine Light should have shone from Arabia last of all had been pre-destined by Divine Wisdom. The purpose behind this can be easily explained. The Arabs are descended from Ishmael whom God had cast forth into the wilderness of Paran,[1] and thus He cut off all connections of this

---

1. From the Arabic word *fārān*, meaning the "two fugitives".

race with the seed of Israel. It was destined that those whom Abraham had cast off from himself should have had no share in the Law of Israel, as it has been said that Ishmael shall not be heir with Isaac. The Ishmaelites were, consequently, isolated from those who were their next of kin and had no relations with any other people. In all other countries, we meet with traces of laws and doctrines preached by prophets — a fact clearly indicating that those nations had, at one time or other, received their teachings from God — but Arabia does not seem to have benefitted by such teachings.

So far as the influence of the prophets is concerned, the Ishmaelites were the most backward people. This act of a wise Providence could not be purposeless. Why were the Ishmaelites kept aloof from the whole world and cut off from the prophecy of Israel? The answer is irresistible. Arabia was destined to be the final scene of prophetic law-giving and the mission of its Prophet was destined to be universal. He came last of all and, therefore, he came to bless all the nations, and rectify the errors of every people. The transcendent knowledge which he gave to the world is perfect in every respect. The Heavenly Law revealed through him aims at the complete reformation of men without any distinction of creed or colour. Its injunctions are in no way meant for one community; on the contrary, it fully deals with all the stages of reformation suited for any people. It gives a universal code, furnishing rules for the civilizing of all men.

To root out a few vices from among a particular community had been the aim of all previous Scriptures, but the Quran set before itself the grand and all-absorbing object of supplying a true remedy for all sorts of evil and gives directions for the guidance of all men. Moreover, it describes all the steps necessary for the social, moral and spiritual development of men. It had first to contend with savageness and raise men to the dignity of social beings by inculcating social virtues. The next step was to preach the higher moral doctrines.

The credit of pointing out the true distinction between natural inclinations and moral qualities is also due to the Quran. But it does not stop with the teaching of excellent morals; it aims at raising men a step higher to the perfection of humanity. It not only opens the door to Divine knowledge, to the certainty concerning God's existence, but also raises men to spiritual excellence. It has enlightened millions of men regarding the true knowledge of God, and established them upon a firm foundation with respect to the certainty of His existence. It gives admirable directions with regard to the threefold advancement of man, which has been discussed above. As the Quran is a comprehensive code of teachings and a guidance relating to the perfection of man, it asserts that claim in the following words:

اَلْيَوْمَ اَكْمَلْتُ لَكُمْ دِيْنَكُمْ وَاَتْمَمْتُ عَلَيْكُمْ نِعْمَتِىْ وَ رَضِيْتُ لَكُمُ الْاِسْلَامَ دِيْنًا

"This day have I perfected for you your religion and completed My favour to you and chosen for you Islam as a religion " — 5 : 3.

This verse lays down clearly that religion attains its perfection in Islam. In other words, upon reaching a stage in which, as signified by the word *Islám*,[1] a person completely submits himself to the will of God, he seeks salvation by the sacrifice of his own self, and not by any other method, and does not allow this sacrifice to remain a mere matter of theory, but demonstrates it in his deeds and practice.

The philosophers who trusted in their imperfect reason could not discover the real God. A true knowledge of His existence was given by the Quran, which suggests two methods of attaining to this knowledge: firstly, it teaches the course by adopting which human reason is strengthened and sharpened in deducing God's existence from the laws of Nature and is protected from falling into

---

1.　Note that *Islám* literally means "submission" or "peace".

error; secondly, it points out the spiritual method, which has been discussed earlier.

Under the first heading, the Holy Book has adduced clear and cogent arguments appealing to human reason in support of the existence of God:

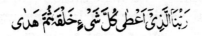

"Our Lord is He Who gives to everything its creation, then guides (it)" — 20 : 50.

Now, if we look to the nature of all creatures from man downward, and consider their constitutions and moulds, we shall find the creation of all things surprisingly adapted to their natures. To enter into any detail upon this point would be trying the patience of the reader. But everyone can think volumes for himself on this subject.

Another argument in support of the existence of God is deduced by the Quran from His being the cause of causes or the first cause:

وَأَنَّ إِلَىٰ رَبِّكَ ٱلْمُنتَهَىٰ

"And that to thy Lord is the goal" — 53 : 42.

This argument is based upon the natural order of cause and effect which pervades the universe. The growth of knowledge and science is the result of the universal dominion of this order over every part of the world, and important laws and principles have been developed out of it. Every cause, which is not itself primary, may be traced to some other cause and this to another, and so on. But as the series of cause and effect taking its rise in this finite world of ours cannot be indefinite, it must terminate at some point. The final cause is, therefore, the Author of the universe. It is to this first or final cause that the verse quoted above calls attention.

Another argument supporting the existence of the Lord is thus described by the Holy Book:

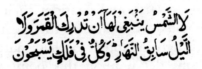

"Neither is it for the sun to overtake the moon, nor can the night outstrip the day. And all float on in an orbit " — 36 : 40.

Had all these heavenly systems no designer, they would soon have been disorganized and destroyed. The vast masses of matter rolling in space, without disturbing each other, demonstrate, by the regularity of their motions, contrivance and design, hence the Designer. It is not at all surprising that these innumerable spheres, thus rolling on from time immemorial, do neither collide, nor alter their courses in the slightest degree, nor are subject to waste or decay from their constant motion. How could such a grand machinery work on without any disorder for numberless years unless it were in accordance with the contrivance and design of a Supreme Contriver? Alluding to this consummate Divine wisdom, the Quran says:

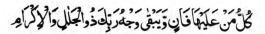

"Is there doubt about Allāh, the Maker of the heavens and the earth?" — 14 : 10.

Another argument relating to the existence of the Creator is thus put forth by the Holy Book:

كُلُّ مَنْ عَلَيْهَا فَانٍ وَيَبْقٰى وَجْهُ رَبِّكَ ذُو الْجَلَالِ وَالْإِكْرَامِ

"Everyone on it passes away—And there endures for ever the person of thy Lord" — 55 : 26-27.

If we suppose the earth reduced to nothing and the heavenly bodies all brought to destruction and the whole material universe made non-existent, still reason and conscience require that something should remain, which should never die nor be ever subject to change or decay. Such a Being is God Who brought everything into existence from nothing.

In another place, the Quran has the following argument in support of the existence of God:

اَلَسْتُ بِرَبِّكُمْ قَالُوْا بَلٰى

"Am I not your Lord? They said: Yes"—7:172.

In this verse, God relates in the form of a dialogue a characteristic of the soul which He has implanted in its nature: that it is not in the nature of the soul to deny the existence of the Divine Being. The atheist rejects the existence of God, not because his nature revolts against it, but because he thinks that he has no proof of His existence. Notwithstanding this denial, he would admit that every effect has also a corresponding cause. No sane person holds that a certain disease, for instance, is not attributable to any cause. A denial of the system of cause and effect overthrows all principles and all sciences. All sorts of calculations which determine the times of eclipses, storms, earthquakes, etc., and all other inferences would become impossible if every effect were not due to a particular cause.

A philosopher, though denying the existence of God, cannot dispute the existence of the first cause as he cannot reject the whole system of the universe. Besides, if a person who denies the existence of God were reduced to a state in which he could be purged of all desires and motives, he would, in this state, admit the existence of God as experience has so often proved. The verse quoted above thus tells us that a denial of His existence is persisted in only so long as the lower desires of man have the upper hand, and that pure nature is strongly impressed with the fact of His existence.

Attributes of God

We shall now consider the attributes of the Almighty Being as taught by the Quran. The following are only a few examples on this subject:

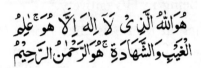

"He is Allāh besides Whom there is no God: The Knower of the unseen and the seen; He is the Beneficent, the Merciful" — 59 : 22.

The idea of a partner with God is negatived because, if He had a rival, His Divinity would be liable at some time to pass wholly to that rival. Further, the words "there is no one besides Him (to be worshipped)" signify that He is a perfect God Whose attributes, beauties and excellences are so high and exalted that if we were to select a god from among other beings, whose selection depended upon the perfection of his attributes, or if we were to suppose certain qualities as the highest and most excellent Divine attributes, nothing would approach Him in His perfection. Injustice could go no further than to set up a partner or a rival with such a Being.

The next attribute, mentioned in the verse above, is that God is "the Knower of the unseen and the seen". No one can comprehend His person with limited human faculties. We can understand everything that has been created, for instance, the sun, the moon, the stars, etc., in its entirety, but we cannot comprehend the Almighty Being in His entirety.[1]

Another attribute is that God provides, out of His bountiful mercy, and not in return for anything done by the creatures, all the means of happiness for all living beings before their creation. We see the manifestation of this attribute in His creation of the sun, the moon, the stars and numerous other things for the benefit of men before they or their deeds ever existed. This gift is due to His attribute of mercy, and it is when this attribute is at work that He is called "the Beneficent" (*al-Raḥmān*).

With respect to another attribute, He is called "the Merciful" (*al-Raḥīm*) — He gives a good reward for the good deeds of His creatures and does not waste any one's effort.

It may be noted that God is also described as "Master of the day of Requital" (*Mālik*

---

1. The verse then goes on to say that "God knows everything, and nothing lies hidden from Him". It would be inconsistent with His Divinity that He should be ignorant of His own creation. He alone can look to every small particle of the universe. He alone knows when He will put an end to this system and bring a general destruction over all things. He alone knows the time of all happenings.

al-Yaumiddin)[1]. He Himself judges the world. He has not made over the dominion of earth and heavens to anybody, nor has He entrusted the right of judgment to any particular person.

He is also "the King" (*al-Malik*), "the Holy" (*al-Quddūs*)[2], Who is without a fault or deficiency. His kingdom is not like earthly kingdoms which may pass into other hands or cease to exist of themselves. The subjects may all emigrate to another country and thus leave a ruler without anything to rule over. A widespread famine may reduce a ruler to something less than a beggar. If the subjects, as a body, rise against the monarch and contest his superiority to rule over them, he may have to give up the reins of monarchy. Such is not, however, the kingdom of God. He has the power to destroy the whole creation and bring new creatures into existence. Had He not been Omnipotent, He would have been obliged to have recourse to injustice in His dealings with His creatures. The salvation of the whole of His first creation would have necessitated the injustice of sending them back to this world to be tried again. If He had no power to create new souls, the world would either have been left without any soul or He would have been obliged to take back the salvation which He had first granted. Either of these courses

---

1. The Quran, 1: 3.   2. *Ibid.*, 59: 23.

would not have been consistent with Divine perfection and, if adopted, would have placed the Lord on a level with imperfect earthly rulers.[1]

The next attribute is contained in His name *al-Salām* — the real "Author of peace"[2], Who is Himself free from every defect, adversity and hardship, and provides safety for others. The significance of this attribute is evident for, if He Himself had been a prey to suffering and adversity, persecuted by men, or unable to carry out His own designs, no heart would ever have looked up to Him in trials and afflictions with the hope of deliverance. Thus He says of false deities:

اِنَّ الَّذِيْنَ تَدْعُوْنَ مِنْ دُوْنِ اللّٰهِ لَنْ يَّخْلُقُوْا
ذُبَابًا وَّلَوِ اجْتَمَعُوْا لَهٗ ۖ وَاِنْ يَّسْلُبْهُمُ الذُّبَابُ شَيْئًا
لَّا يَسْتَنْقِذُوْهُ مِنْهُ ۗ ضَعُفَ الطَّالِبُ وَالْمَطْلُوْبُ ۝
مَا قَدَرُوا اللّٰهَ حَقَّ قَدْرِهٖ ۗ اِنَّ اللّٰهَ لَقَوِيٌّ عَزِيْزٌ ۝

"Surely those whom you call upon besides Allāh cannot create a fly, though they should all gather for it. And if the fly carry off aught from them,

---

1. Note that the laws which governments make for the management of their affairs can be defective and, when obliged to have recourse to measures of oppression and injustice, they look upon them as being based on principles of justice and equity. Temporal governments, for instance, deem it justifiable that a boat should sink with its crew when it is likely to collide with a ship and thus liable to cause a greater loss of life and property. But it is not consistent with the idea of Divinity that God

they cannot take it back from it. Weak are
(both) the invoker and the invoked. They
estimate not Allāh with His due estimation.
Surely Allāh is Strong, Mighty " — 22 : 73-74.

Yet another attribute is *al-Mu'min* — "the
Granter of Security"[1] — the establisher of arguments in support of His unity and excellence.
This attribute calls attention to the fact that a
believer in the true God may consider himself
safe on every occasion. He is not ashamed before
people because he has strong and cogent arguments
in support of his assertions. But the worshipper
of a false deity is always in trouble. Having no
argument in his favour, he takes any assertion
which is contrary to reason for a deep mystery, so
that under that name his errors may pass for
something transcending human reason.

The following verses may be quoted to illus-
trate some more attributes of God:

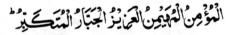

"(Allāh is) Guardian over all, the Mighty, the

---

should be driven to an extremity in which the adoption of one or two
defective courses should become inevitable. If He had not the power
to create every thing from nothing, we can only liken Him to the ruler
of a petty state who must either use oppression to keep up his divinity or,
being just, be left without a world to rule over. But the Almighty is free
from every such defect, and the mighty ship of His power floats upon the
ocean of justice and equity.

2. The Quran, 59: 23.   1. *Ibid.*

Supreme, the Possessor of greatness" — 59:23.

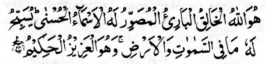

"He is Allāh, the Creator, the Shaper out
of naught, the Fashioner: His are the most
beautiful names. Whatever is in the heavens
and the earth declares His glory; and
He is the Mighty, the Wise"[1] — 59 : 24.

اِنَّ اللّٰہَ عَلٰی کُلِّ شَیْءٍ قَدِیْرٌ

"Lo! Allāh is Able to do all things"[2] — 2 : 148.

اُجِیْبُ دَعْوَۃَ الدَّاعِ اِذَا دَعَانِ

"I (Allāh) answer the prayer of the suppliant
when he calls on Me ... "   — 2 : 186.

رَبِّ الْعٰلَمِیْنَ ۞ الرَّحْمٰنِ
الرَّحِیْمِ ۞ مٰلِکِ یَوْمِ الدِّیْنِ ۞

"The Lord[3] of the worlds, the Beneficent, the

---

1. This verse indicates that there are inhabitants in the heavenly bodies
who follow Divine rules of guidance.
2. This is the real source of comfort for the worshippers of the true God,
for how could man centre all his hopes in Him if He Himself were weak?
3. There is no single word in English carrying the significance of the
Arabic word *Rabb*—"Nourisher unto perfection" would be nearest; but
the word *Lord* has been adopted for the sake of brevity — Publisher.

Merciful, Master of the day of Requital"—1 :2-4.

الْحَیُّ الْقَیُّومُ

"(Allāh is) the Ever-living . . . "[1] — 3 : 2.

قُلْ هُوَ اللّٰهُ أَحَدٌ ۞ اللّٰهُ الصَّمَدُ ۞ لَمْ یَلِدْ هُ وَلَمْ
یُولَدْ ۞ وَلَمْ یَكُنْ لَّهُ كُفُوًا اَحَدٌ ۞

"Say: He, Allāh, is One. Allāh is He on Whom all depend. He begets not, nor is He begotten; and none is like Him" — 112 : 1-4.

It should be borne in mind that justice in relation to the Creator consists in being firmly established upon the true path of Divine Unity without deviating a hair's breadth from it at all. The moral injunctions, to which attention has already been called, form a part of the ethical teachings of the Quran. The most conspicuous feature of all these teachings is perfect freedom from excess and default. The Holy Book does not categorize any quality as a moral quality unless it is exercised within its proper limits. It need not be demonstrated that virtue lies in the middle course: it is a mean between two extremes. Whatever inclines a man to the middle path and establishes him in the mean course is conducive to good morals. The man who acts on the right

---

1. This verse excludes all notions of the death of God.

occasion follows the mean path which alone can lead to good. The farmer who scatters seed upon his fields either too late or too early departs, in so doing, from the middle path and the result is a waste of seed. Virtue, truth and wisdom lie in the middle path and he only can walk in that path who watches for the opportunity.

Between two falsehoods, which occupy either extreme, lies the middle course, the path of truth which can be kept only by the observance of the right occasion. As in other moral qualities, the middle path must be adhered to in the recognition of the existence of the Lord. The mean in this consists in avoiding, on the one hand, the view which divests the Divine Being of every attribute and in rejecting, on the other, the view which likens Him to material things. This is the position which the Quran has taken with regard to the attributes of the Almighty. It recognizes Him as Seeing, Hearing, Speaking, Knowing, etc., but cautions us at the same time not to liken Him to anything which our senses can comprehend:

لَيْسَ كَمِثْلِهِ شَيْءٌ

"Naught is as His likeness . . . " — 42 : 11.

فَلَا تَضْرِبُوا لِلّٰهِ الْأَمْثَالَ

"So coin not similitudes for Allāh" — 16 : 74.

Such is the true conception of God! Islam adopts the golden mean in all its teachings. The opening chapter of the Holy Book inculcates the adoption of the mean path when it teaches :

اِهۡدِنَا الصِّرَاطَ الۡمُسۡتَقِیۡمَ ۞ صِرَاطَ الَّذِیۡنَ اَنۡعَمۡتَ عَلَیۡهِمۡ ۚ۬ غَیۡرِ الۡمَغۡضُوۡبِ عَلَیۡهِمۡ وَلَا الضَّآلِّیۡنَ ۞

"Guide us on the right path, the path of those upon whom Thou hast bestowed favours,[1] not those upon whom wrath is brought down, nor those who go astray " — 1 : 6-7.

In this verse, three kinds of people have been mentioned. First of all, there are the *maghḍūb ʿalaihim* by which the Holy Book alludes to people who assume an attitude of wilful disobedience towards God and thus, following their own savage inclinations, call down the Divine wrath upon themselves. Then are the *ḍāllīn* by which are intended people who are led astray by following their bestial inclinations and their delusions. Midway between these two extremes are the people who walk in the right (middle) path and whom the Quran denominates *anʿamta ʿalaihim*. In fact, to direct people in the middle path is the one

---

1.   It is in the footsteps of the prophets, the truthful, the faithful and the righteous that the Muslim aspires to walk — Publisher.

object of the Holy Book. Moses laid stress upon
retaliation and Jesus upon forbearance, but the
Quran teaches the use of both in their proper
place. Elsewhere, we read the following:

وَكَذَٰلِكَ جَعَلْنَاكُمْ أُمَّةً وَّسَطًا

"And thus We (Allāh) have (indeed) made
you an exalted nation ..." — 2 : 143.

Blessed are those people who adopt this
course for, as the Arabic proverb says: the golden
mean is the best!

C. Spiritual Conditions

It has already been stated that the source of
the spiritual conditions is the *nafs al-muṭma'inna*
(soul at rest), which takes a man onward in his
moral progress and makes him godly, transports
him from the moral to the spiritual field:

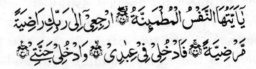

"O Soul that art at rest, return to thy Lord, well
pleased, well-pleasing, so enter among My
servants, and enter My Garden ! — 89 : 27-30

These verses have a plain bearing upon the
spiritual conditions of man.

Heavenly life

In discussing the spiritual conditions, it is necessary to comment upon the above verses in some detail. The highest spiritual condition to which man can aspire in this world is that he should rest contented with God and should find his quietude, his happiness and his delight in Him alone. This is the stage of life which we term the "heavenly life". The pure and perfect sincerity, truth and righteousness of a person are rewarded by the Almighty by granting him a heaven upon this earth. All others look to a prospective paradise, but such a one enters paradise in this very life. It is at this stage, too, that a person realizes that the prayers and worship, which at first appeared to him as a burden, are really a nourishment on which the growth of his soul depends and that this is the basis of his spiritual development. He then sees that the fruit of his efforts is not to be reaped in a future life only.

The spirit which, in the second stage, although blaming a man for the impurities of life, was yet powerless to resist evil tendencies or to blot them out wholly, and too infirm to establish a man upon the principles of virtue with firmness, now reaches a stage of development in which its efforts are crowned with success. The sensual passions die out of themselves and the soul no more stumbles but, strengthened with the Divine spirit, is ashamed

of its past failings. The state of struggle with evil
propensities is left behind. An entire change
passes over the nature of man and his former habits
undergo a complete transformation. He is perfectly estranged from his former course of life. He
is washed of all impurities and perfectly cleansed.
The Lord Himself plants the love of virtue in his
heart and purifies it of the defilement of evil.
The hosts of truth encamp in his heart and righteousness controls all its powers. Truth is now
victorious and falsehood lays down its arms
and is reduced to subjection. It is to this state
that the following verses of the Holy Quran point:

أُولَٰئِكَ كَتَبَ فِي قُلُوبِهِمُ الْإِيمَانَ وَأَيَّدَهُم بِرُوحٍ مِّنْهُ

He has impressed faith, and strengthened them
with a Spirit from Himself . . . " —58 : 22.

جَاءَ الْحَقُّ وَزَهَقَ الْبَاطِلُ إِنَّ الْبَاطِلَ كَانَ زَهُوقًا

"The Truth has come and falsehood vanished.
Surely falsehood is ever bound to vanish"—17:81.

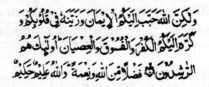

"Allāh has endeared the faith to you and has

made it seemly in your hearts, and He has made
hateful to you disbelief and transgression and
disobedience. Such are those who are rightly
guided — a grace from Allāh and a favour.
And Allāh is Knowing, Wise" — 49 : 7-8.

Such are the words of the Quran relating to
the third stage of the advancement of the spirit!
The person who has not realized this state is without
true sight. We must mark the words that God
engraved faith upon the hearts of believers with
His own hand and strengthened them with the
Holy Spirit. These words can bear no other
significance than this: that the attainment of true
purity and righteousness is impossible except
through heavenly help.

In the second stage of the spirit, which we have
termed the "self-accusing spirit", there is a struggle
between good and evil tendencies. A person feels
the compunctions of his good nature for a time but
evil propensities again get the upper hand. He is
conscious of his fall and sometimes even despairs
of reformation and of complete victory of his good
nature over evil tendencies. When the period
of his spiritual struggle is over, a light descends
upon him accompanied with Divine strength. The
descent of this light works a wonderful transformation in his soul and he feels a strong, invisible hand
leading him onward. A new world discloses

itself to his sight and he then witnesses the existence of God. His eyes are brightened with a new light and things are revealed to him which he was hitherto unable to see.

Divine blessings

But how can we discover this path and how can we acquire this light? No effect can be produced without a cause, no end is attained without adopting the means thereto, and no knowledge is obtained without treading along the path leading to it. The laws of Nature cannot be broken. They amply testify that to achieve a result there is a right course, and that its attainment is dependent upon the adoption of that particular course. If we are sitting in a dark room and need the light of the sun,

we are to open the door facing the sun. In like manner, there must be a door through which the blessings and favours of the Merciful can be received and a method by which the spiritual state can be attained. Therefore, it is our duty to seek this right path for our spiritual welfare, as we are engaged day and night in search of means which are calculated to better our physical and temporal state.

But the question is whether that path can be discovered by the efforts of reason alone, and whether we can successfully seek a union in God by the sole ingenuity of our own mind. Is it true that mere logic and philosophy can open for us the doors which experience tells us can only be opened by the powerful hand of God? No, mere human devices can never reveal to us the shining face of the living and supporting Almighty. Let him who would walk on the right path completely submit himself with all his faculties and powers to the will of the Beneficent and then pray unceasingly and untiringly for the Divine union and thus realize the reality of the existence of God through Divine assistance.

The most excellent prayer in this respect, put in appropriate words, and adopted best to meet the requirements of human nature — drawing at the same time a faithful picture of the natural zeal of the soul — is that taught by the Holy Book in its opening chapter, called *al-Faliḥa*:

بِسْمِ اللهِ الرَّحْمٰنِ الرَّحِيمِ ۞

اَلْحَمْدُ لِلّٰهِ رَبِّ الْعٰلَمِينَ ۞ الرَّحْمٰنِ

الرَّحِيمِ ۞ مٰلِكِ يَوْمِ الدِّينِ ۞

اِيَّاكَ نَعْبُدُ وَاِيَّاكَ نَسْتَعِينُ ۞

اِهْدِنَا الصِّرَاطَ الْمُسْتَقِيمَ ۞ صِرَاطَ

الَّذِينَ اَنْعَمْتَ عَلَيْهِمْ غَيْرِ

الْمَغْضُوبِ عَلَيْهِمْ وَلَا الضَّآلِّينَ ۞

"In the name of Allāh, the Beneficent, the Merciful. Praise be to Allāh, the Lord of the

worlds, the Beneficent, the Merciful, Master
of the day of Requital. Thee do we[1] serve
and Thee do we beseech for help. Guide
us on the right path, the path of those upon
whom Thou hast bestowed favours, not (the
path) of those upon whom wrath is brought
down, nor those who go astray" — 1:1-7.

It is clear from these verses that the blessings
of the Beneficent descend upon persons who
sacrifice their lives and all their interests in His
path, make a complete submission to Him and
resign themselves wholly to His will and then
supplicate Him to grant them all the spiritual
blessings to which man can attain of nearness and
union with Him, and of speaking to, and being
addressed by Him. These persons engage all
their faculties in devotion to God, eschew every
form of disobedience and prostrate themselves
before Him. They shun every evil course and
avoid occasions of His wrath. They seek the
Creator with true sincerity and exalted magnani-
mity and their efforts are, therefore, crowned
with success, and they are made to drink of the
cup of Divine knowledge.

This first chapter of the Quran further refers
to constancy in the path of God, thus indicating
that the Divine blessings, which bring about the

---

1 The use of the plural "we" indicates that all the faculties are engaged
in Divine worship and working in complete submission to the Lord for
man, considered with reference to his internal faculties, is regarded not
as an individual but as a class. This total resignation of all faculties
to the will of God is the true significance of the word *Islām*.

spiritual state, do not flow in their fullness until a
person shows firmness and sincerity unshaken
under the severest trials.   He must have a union
which cannot be cut asunder by a sword nor
burnt by fire: adversity cannot loosen the tie,
the death of the nearest relatives has not the
slightest effect upon it, the separation of dear
objects does not interfere with it and the most
fearful calamities do not shake it.   Narrow is the
door indeed and difficult the path. Ah, what
a mountain to ascend! The following Quranic
verse calls attention to this very difficult point:

قُلْ إِنْ كَانَ آبَاؤُكُمْ وَأَبْنَاؤُكُمْ وَإِخْوَانُكُمْ وَأَزْوَاجُكُمْ
وَعَشِيرَتُكُمْ وَأَمْوَالٌ اقْتَرَفْتُمُوهَا وَتِجَارَةٌ تَخْشَوْنَ
كَسَادَهَا وَمَسَاكِنُ تَرْضَوْنَهَا أَحَبَّ إِلَيْكُمْ مِنَ اللَّهِ وَ
رَسُولِهِ وَجِهَادٍ فِي سَبِيلِهِ فَتَرَبَّصُوا حَتَّى يَأْتِيَ اللَّهُ
بِأَمْرِهِ وَاللَّهُ لَا يَهْدِي الْقَوْمَ الْفَاسِقِينَ ۝

"Say: If your fathers and your sons and your
brethren and your wives and your kinsfolk and
the wealth you have acquired, and trade whose
dullness you fear, and dwellings you love,
are dearer to you than Allāh and His Messenger
and striving in His way, then wait till Allāh
brings His command to pass. And Allāh
guides not the transgressing people" — 9 : 24.

This is the third stage of advancement and it
is on reaching this stage that a person becomes
godly, provided he is willing to subject himself to
every affliction for the sake of the Lord, and turns
to Him with such exclusive devotion and sincerity
as to regard all beside Him as dead.

The truth is that it is impossible for us to see
the Lord unless a death comes first over all our
passions and desires. The day on which such a
death overtakes our earthly life is the day of the
triumph of spirituality and the day of the Divine
revelation. We are blind so long as we are not
blind to all other sights, and we are lifeless so long
as we are not lifeless under the hand of God.
The uprightness which enables us to overcome all
carnal passions is granted to us only when we are
directly facing the Creator. Uprightness deals a
death-blow to all carnal desires, and it is to this
state that the following words call attention:

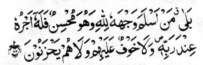

"Nay, whoever submits himself entirely to
Allāh and he is the doer of good (to others), he
has his reward from his Lord, and there is no fear
for such nor shall they grieve" — 2 : 112.

This stage of uprightness is not attained until
all the members of our body and all the faculties

which sustain us begin to work in total submission
to the Almighty, and our life and death have no
other object but the pleasure of the Merciful:

قُلْ اِنَّ صَلَاتِى وَ نُسُكِى وَ مَحْيَاىَ وَ مَمَاتِى لِلّٰهِ رَبِّ الْعٰلَمِينَ

"Say: My prayer and my sacrifice and my
life and my death are surely for Allāh,
the   Lord   of   the   Worlds " — 6 : 163.

When man's love for the Creator is so great,
when his life and death have no interest for himself
but are solely for the sake of God, then the Lord,
Who loves those who love Him, causes His love to
descend upon that person.   From the union of
these two loves springs up a light which cannot be
perceived or realized by those who are bent low
upon this earth.   Thousands of the faithful and
righteous have been murdered in cold blood by
the worldly-minded because the world was blind
to the light which had descended upon them.
They were looked upon as covetous and deceitful
contrivers, for it could not see their bright faces.
The Word of God attests to this spiritual blindness
in the following words:

وَ تَرٰىهُمْ يَنْظُرُونَ اِلَيْكَ وَ هُمْ لَا يُبْصِرُونَ

"And thou (the Prophet) seest them looking
towards thee, yet they see not" — 7 : 198.

An earthly person, therefore, becomes a heavenly

being when illumined by the celestial light. The
Author of all existence speaks with him and
illumines him with the lustre of Divinity. His
heart, which overflows with the love of his Divine
Master, becomes God's habitation and the throne
of His glory. From the moment that such a man
is renewed, having undergone a pure transformation, the Almighty also becomes new to him for
His dealings and laws with him are changed.
Not that the Creator becomes new or His laws and
dealings are new but that these laws and dealings
are distinct from those displayed in connection
with the mass of men, and are such as the worldly
wise are not cognizant of. It is to such transformation that the following Quranic verse refers:

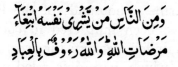

"And of men is he who would sell' himself
to seek the pleasure of Allāh. And Allāh
is Compassionate to the servants " — 2 : 207.

Such is the case of the person who has attained
the spiritual stage of perfection! In the above
verse, we are told that the mercy of the Almighty
encompasses such a person and, consequently, he
alone is delivered from all suffering and sin who
gives himself away in the right path and Divine
pleasure and, with this sacrifice, gives proof of his
exclusive devotion. He regards himself as having

been created for no other purpose but obedience
to the Lord and sympathy for His creatures.
When he has thus submitted his will and intention
to the will of God, every faculty is engaged in the
performance of pure virtue, not formally or coldly
but with sincere interest, zeal and pleasure as
though actually seeing his Master in the mirror
of his obedience and submission.   The will of God
becomes his will and he has no delight but in
obedience to Him.   He does not perform good or
virtuous deeds simply on account of their goodness
but his very nature is drawn in that direction and
he finds his highest pleasure and bliss in them.
This is the paradise upon earth which is granted
to the spiritual man, and the promised heaven
in the next world is only an image of the present
paradise, being an embodiment of the spiritual
blessings which such a man enjoys down here.
Referring to this, the Holy Book says:

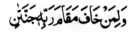

"And for him who fears to stand before

---

1. In this verse, the word *kāfūr* (camphor) is derived, as already indicated,
from *kafr* (to suppress; to cover), and refers to the total extinction of worldly
love and the complete suppression of all worldly desires of those who have
drunk of the cup of the love of God and severance of all other connections
with true sincerity.   It is clear that passions take their growth in the
heart, and if the heart is removed farther off from impurities, passions
gradually lessen and ultimately die out.   The more a man leans towards
the Almighty, the farther off he is from the control of carnal passions, and
therefore the righteous who trust in Him alone for support have their
hearts cleansed from the fire of passion, and their sensual desires are as
completely suppressed as poisonous matter is washed out by camphor.

his Lord are two Gardens " — 55 : 46.

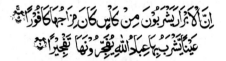

"And their Lord makes them (the righteous
people) to drink a pure drink " — 76 : 21.

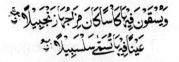

"The righteous shall truly drink of a cup
tempered with camphor[1] — a fountain from
which the (faithful) servants of Allāh drink,
making it flow in abundance " — 76 : 5-6.

"And they (the righteous) are made to drink
therein a cup tempered with ginger[1] — (of) a
fountain therein called Salsabīl " — 76 : 17-18.

---

1. *Zanjabil* (ginger) is a compound of *zanā* and *jabl*. Of these component
parts, the first means "to ascend" and the second "mountain". The
compound word *zanjabil* therefore means "he ascended the mountain."
Now, from a severe attack of a poisonous disease to perfect restoration of
health, there are two stages. In the first, the poisonous germs are completely destroyed, the violence of the attack is mitigated and the danger
which threatened life itself is over. But the weakness which is the result
of the attack does not vanish with the poison. The patient, though out of
danger, cannot be said to be in sound health until strength is restored
to him. If he stumbles and falls, he is not yet a healthy person. The
second stage of restoration is that in which the patient regains his strength.
The body is again full of life and vigour, and he is not only able to walk

اِنَّآ اَعۡتَدۡنَا لِلۡكٰفِرِیۡنَ سَلٰسِلَا۠ وَاَغۡلٰلًا وَّسَعِیۡرًا ۞

"Surely We have prepared for the disbelievers
chains and shackles and a burning Fire"—76: 4.

This verse signifies that those who do not seek
God with a pure heart are, by Divine law, repaid
in their own coin.   Their entanglements in worldly
affairs do not allow them to move a step as though
their feet had been enchained; they are bent so
low upon the mean cares of the world that they
appear to have collars round their necks which
do not allow them to raise their heads heaven-
ward; their hearts burn with carnal desires and
greed to gain property or to overthrow a rival.
Since the Almighty finds them indulging in low
desires and unfit for higher and sublimer pursuits,

with firm legs upon even ground, but has courage and strength to try
the ascent of a steep mountain and scale the heights cheerfully and without
fear.   This is the spiritual state which a person attains in the third stage
of development.   It is in reference to this stage that God says to the
righteous that they are made to drink of a cup tempered with zanjabīl.

The two above quoted verses in which kāfūr and zanjabīl are spoken of
call attention to the two stages through which a person must pass in order
to make an advance from the low position of slavery of passion to the
heights of virtue and righteousness.   After the first movement which a
man makes to rise, the first stage is that in which poisonous matters are
suppressed and the flood of passions begins to subside.   This we may
term the kāfūr (suppressing) stage for, in this stage, what is effected is only
the suppression of poisonous matters just as kāfūr has the property of
nullifying the effect of poison.   But the strength which is required to
overcome all difficulties is only acquired in the second stage, called the
zanjabīl (strengthening) stage.   The spiritual zanjabīl, which has the effect
of a tonic on the spiritual system, is the manifestation of Divine glory which
afford nourishment to the soul.   Braced with this manifestation, man is
able to traverse the dreary deserts and climb the steep heights which the
spiritual wayfarer must pass to reach the goal.   The wonderful deeds of
self-sacrifice that he is then able to perform are beyond the comprehension
of those whose hearts are devoid of the zeal of love.

He makes these three afflictions their consant
companions: chains, collars and fire.

There is also allusion here to the fact that
every deed which a man does is followed by a
corresponding act of God.   If a man, for instance,
closes all the doors of his room, the darkness that
follows is a Divine act.   In fact, whatever we
term the natural consequences of our deeds are
really the deeds of the Lord, for He is the cause
of causes.   The taking of poison is a man's own
deed but this is followed by Divine punishment
with death.   As in the material world, so too in
the spiritual, the law holds good that whatever
is done is followed by a necessary consequence.
The following verses are quoted to show how this
law is referred to in different instances:

فَلَمَّا زَاغُوٓا اَزَاغَ اللّٰهُ قُلُوۡبَهُمۡ

"But when they (people of Moses) deviated,
Allāh made their hearts deviate. . ." — 61 : 5.

وَالَّذِيۡنَ جَاهَدُوۡا فِيۡنَا لَنَهۡدِيَنَّهُمۡ سُبُلَنَا

"And those who strive hard for Us, We shall
certainly guide them in Our ways . . ." — 29:69.

وَمَنۡ كَانَ فِىۡ هٰذِهٖٓ اَعۡمٰى فَهُوَ فِى الۡاٰخِرَةِ اَعۡمٰى وَاَضَلُّ سَبِيۡلًا

"And whoever is blind in this (very world)

he will be blind in the Hereafter, and
further away from the (right) path" — 17 : 72.

This clearly indicates that it is in this life that
the righteous see the Merciful, and that it is in this
very life that He appears to them in all His majesty
and glory. In short, it is down here that a
heavenly life begins and it is in this very world,
and not hereafter, that the basis of a hellish life is
laid in the impurities of this life and blindness
to spiritual realities. Another verse suns thus:

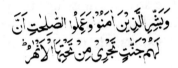

"And give good news to those who believe and
do good deeds, that for them are Gardens
underneath which rivers flow . . . " — 2 : 25.

In these words, God compares belief to gardens
beneath which rivers flow. They reveal a secret
indicating the connection between faith and good
deeds. As trees would wither away if they were
not watered, so faith without good deeds is dead.
Faith without deeds is useless, and good deeds not
actuated by faith are a mere show. The Islamic
paradise is a true representation of the faith and
good deeds of this world. Every man's paradise
is an image of what he has done here below. It
does not come from without, but grows from
within a man himself. It is his own faith and his

own good deeds that take the form of a paradise for him to live in, and its delight is tasted in this very life. The tree of faith and the streams of good deeds are even here discernible though not manifest; but in the next life all veils that hide them from the eye shall be uplifted and their existence shall be palpably felt. The teaching of the Quran tells us that true, pure, strong and perfect faith in God, His attributes and His will is a delightful orchard, while the good deeds which a man does are, in fact, the streams flowing in the orchard, giving life and fruit to its trees. The same idea is elsewhere expressed in the following words:

كَلِمَةً طَيِّبَةً كَشَجَرَةٍ طَيِّبَةٍ أَصْلُهَا ثَابِتٌ وَ
فَرْعُهَا فِى السَّمَاءِ ۞ تُؤْتِى أُكُلَهَا كُلَّ حِينٍ

"A good word (being) as a good tree, whose root is firm and whose branches are high, yielding its fruit in every season . . ."—14:24-25.

By comparing a good word of faith to a good tree that ever yields its fruit, God has called attention to three facts: firstly, that its root, which indicates its true significance, should be firmly fixed in the earth which represents the heart of man. The firm fixture of the root indicates the unqualified acceptance of the reality and truth of the faith by the nature and conscience of man; secondly, that its branches should be in heaven, that is, reason should attest to its truth and the heavenly laws of Nature, being the work of the Almighty, should agree with it; that arguments of its truth should be deducible from the laws of Nature and should be so high as if they were in heaven, being above every objection, and thirdly, that it yields its fruit without ceasing, that is, its influence and blessings are never intercepted and are felt in every age and every country. It is not true that they exist for a time and then cease. Another verse then follows:

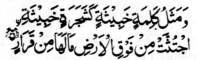

"And the parable of an evil word is like (that of) an evil tree, pulled up from the earth's surface; it has no stability"[1] — 14 : 26.

It will be noted that, as the Quran has compared the words of faith to plants bearing delicious fruits as being embodiments of what is enjoyable in this world, it has also described the evil tree of unbelief under the name of *zaqqūm*. Thus it says:

اَذٰلِكَ خَيْرٌ نُّزُلًا اَمْ شَجَرَةُ الزَّقُّوْمِ ۞ اِنَّا جَعَلْنٰهَا
فِتْنَةً لِّلظّٰلِمِيْنَ ۞ اِنَّهَا شَجَرَةٌ تَخْرُجُ فِيْۤ اَصْلِ
الْجَحِيْمِ ۞ طَلْعُهَا كَاَنَّهُ رُءُوْسُ الشَّيٰطِيْنِ ۞

---

1. It is neither supported by arguments nor by the laws of Nature and is a mere assertion or an idle tale.

"Is this the better entertainment or the tree of Zaqqūm?¹ Surely We have made it a trial for the wrong-doers. It is a tree that springs forth in the bottom of hell — its produce is as it were the heads of serpents" — 37 : 62-65.

ذُقْ اِنَّكَ اَنْتَ الْعَزِيْزُ الْكَرِيْمُ ۞

"Taste (the fruit of this tree) — thou art forsooth the mighty, the honourable ! " — 44 : 49.

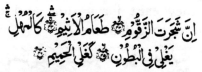

"Surely the tree of Zaqqūm is the food of the sinful; like molten brass, it seethes in (their) bellies like boiling water" — 44: 43-46.

These words indicate that if the sinner had not been self-conceited or had not turned his back upon the Truth for the sake of his pretended honour and greatness, he would not have had to taste that fruit and affliction.

In short, God has likened the words of faith uttered in this world to the trees of paradise, and the words of faithlessness to *zaqqūm*, the tree of hell, and has thus shown that a heavenly or a hellish life commences in this world. Regarding hell, the Holy Book also says:

The cursed tree is the tree of *zaqqūm*. According to the Quran, every good action is a good tree and every evil action is an evil tree. In these verses, we are told that the eating of *zaqqūm* brings damnation and destruction as the result.

نَارُاللّٰهِ الْمُوْقَدَةُ ۞ الَّتِى تَطَّلِعُ عَلَى الْاَفْئِدَةِ ۞

"(It is) the Fire kindled by Allāh,[1] which
rises over the hearts (of men)" — 104 : 6-7.

فَاتَّقُوا النَّارَ الَّتِى وَقُوْدُهَا النَّاسُ وَالْحِجَارَةُ

"Be on your guard against the fire whose
fuel is (of) men and stones . . . " — 2 : 24.

اِنَّكُمْ وَمَا تَعْبُدُوْنَ مِنْ دُوْنِ اللّٰهِ حَصَبُ جَهَنَّمَ

"Surely you (idolaters) and what you worship
besides Allāh are fuel of hell . . . " — 21 : 98.

From these remarks, it would appear that
Heaven and Hell are not material worlds like the
present one but that spiritual facts are their source
and origin. This requires to be qualified in one
way: that the blessings and tortures of the next
world shall be the embodiments of the spiritual
facts of this one but, notwithstanding this, they
shall not be things of this world.

Stage of perfection

Returning to the subject, the Quran has taught
us two means for a perfect spiritual union with
God: complete resignation to His will, which is
known by the name of *Islām*, and constant prayers
and supplications as taught in the opening chapter

---

1. This is an allusion to the fact that the grief sorrow and affliction
which overpower the heart really kindle the fire of hell.

of the Book, known as *Fātiḥa*. These are the two channels which lead to the fountain of salvation and the only safe guides which take us to the Lord. These are the only means to attain the desired end of the highest spiritual advancement and ultimate union with the Almighty. They only can find the Merciful who realise the true significance of *Islām* by actually entering into it, and who pray as taught in the *Fātiḥa*.

What is Islām? It is the burning fire which consumes all our low desires and, setting fire to false gods, makes us offer our life, honour and property as a sacrifice before the Master. Entering into this state, we drink the water of a new life. The spiritual powers within us are united together as strongly as the links of a chain. A fire, resembling that of lighting, flashes out of us and a fire descends from above. These two flames, uniting with each other, consume all low motives and carnal desires and the love of others than the Lord. A sort of death comes over our previous life, and this state is signified by the word *Islām*.

Islam brings about the death of the passions of the flesh and gives new life to us. This is the true regeneration. The holy Word of God must be revealed to the person who reaches this stage, which is termed "union" His connection with the Almighty is so strong that he, as it were, sees Him. He is granted strength from above; the internal faculties are all brightened and the

magnetism of a pure heavenly life works strongly.
Upon reaching this stage, God becomes his eye
with which he sees, his tongue with which he
speaks, his ear with which he hears, his hand with
which he defends himself, and his foot with which
he walks. It is in reference to this stage that
the Holy Book says:

يَدُاللّٰهِ فَوْقَ اَيْدِيهِمْ

"(Those who swear allegiance to Muḥammad
do but swear allegiance to Allāh). The hand
of Allāh is above their hands . . . " — 48 : 10.

وَمَا رَمَيْتَ اِذْ رَمَيْتَ وَلٰكِنَّ اللّٰهَ رَمٰى

"And thou smotest not when thou didst smite
(the enemy), but Allāh smote (him). . . "—8:17.

This is the stage of the perfection of man and
of his union with the Benefactor. The will of
God predominates over every desire and the
moral conditions, which were at first defenceless
against the passions of the flesh, are fortified so as
to be proof against every attack. With this holy
transformation, reason and understanding are also
refined. The Quran refers to this condition :

اُولٰٓئِكَ كَتَبَ فِىْ قُلُوْبِهِمُ الْاِيْمَانَ وَ اَيَّدَهُمْ بِرُوْحٍ مِّنْهُ

"These are they into whose hearts He (Allāh)
has impressed faith, and strengthened them
with a Spirit from Himself . . ." — 58 : 22.

The love of such a person for his Lord knows
no bounds. To die for the Creator and to suffer
persecution or disgrace for His sake, however
strange the expression might sound to other ears,
are to him a matter of course. Being drawn, he
flies towards Him, but does not know what attracts
him. An invisible hand supports him under all
conditions, and to fulfil the will of God becomes
the principal object of his life. He finds himself
close to his Master, as the Quran says:

وَنَحْنُ أَقْرَبُ إِلَيْهِ مِنْ حَبْلِ الْوَرِيدِ

"(And certainly We created man) — and We
are nearer to him than his life-vein" —50 : 16

As no effort is required to pluck a ripened
fruit from a plant, the low connections of such a
man, in like manner, are severed of themselves.
He has a deep relationship with the Almighty
and is removed far off from the creatures. He
speaks with God and is spoken to by Him. To
reach this stage, the doors are as wide open now
as they were in times past. The Divine grace does
not withhold this blessing from earnest seekers
now but vouchsafes it to them as bountifully to-day
as it did in the past:

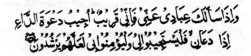

"And when My servants ask thee concerning
Me, surely I am nigh.   I answer the prayer of

the suppliant when he calls on Me, so they
should hear My call and believe in Me that
they may walk in the right way" — 2 : 186.

Difficult is the way and dangerous the path,
and one cannot walk in it as long as one does not
set one's foot with true sincerity upon the burning
fire which others flee from!

LIFE AFTER DEATH

> "And We have made every man's actions to cling to his neck, and We shall bring forth to him on the day of Resurrection a book which he will find wide open . . . " — 17:13.

What is the teaching of the Quran as to the state of man in his life after death, is the next question which offers itself for solution.

Representation by images

The state after death is not altogether a new state; it is in fact a complete representation, a full image of our spiritual state in the present life. Here the good or bad conditions of the deeds or beliefs of a man are latent within him and their poison or panacea casts its influence upon him secretly, but in the life to come they shall become manifest and clear as daylight. An idea of it, although a very imperfect one, may be had from the manner in which a person sees in a

dream the embodiment of whatever is predominent
in his temperament. When he is due for an
attack of fever, he may see in a dream flames of
burning fire, whereas he may find himself in
floods of water when he is about to catch cold.

When the body is prepared for a particular
disease, a dream may often disclose the embodiment of the conditions giving rise to it. From
the manner in which internal conditions are
represented in physical forms, in dreams, we can
have an idea of the embodiment of the spiritual
conditions of this world in the life to come. After
our earthly course is ended, we are translated to
regions where our deeds and their consequences
assume a shape, and what is hidden in us in this
world is there unrolled and laid open before us.
These embodiments of spiritual facts are substantial
realities, as even in dreams, though the sight soon
vanishes away, yet so long as it is before our eyes
it is taken to be reality. As this representation
by images is a new and a perfect manifestation of
the power of God, we may as well call it not a
representation of certain facts, but a new creation
brought about by the powerful hand of the
Creator. With reference to this, the Quran says:

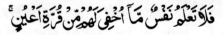

"So no soul knows what refreshment of the
eyes is hidden for them..." — 32 : 17.

Thus the Lord describes the heavenly blessings that the righteous shall enjoy in the next life as having been kept secret because, not being like anything contained in this world, no one knows aught about them. It is evident that the things of this world are not a secret to us; we not only know pomegranates, grapes, milk, etc., but frequently taste of them. Consequently, these things could not be called secrets. The fruits of paradise have, therefore, nothing in common with these except the name. He is indeed ignorant of the Holy Quran who takes paradise for a place where only the things of this world are provided in abundance.

It may be added here, in explanation of the verse quoted above, that Prophet Muḥammad said that heaven and its blessings are things which "the eye hath not seen, nor hath ear heard, nor hath it entered into the heart of man to conceive of them." But of the things of this world we cannot say that our eyes have not seen them, or that our ears have not heard them, or that our minds have not conceived of them. When God and His Prophet tell us of things in heaven which our senses are not cognizant of in this world, we should be guilty of cherishing doctrines against the teachings of the Quran if we supposed rivers flowing with the milk which we ordinarily drink here. Can we, moreover, consistently with the idea of heaven, suppose herds of cows and buffaloes reared in paradise and numerous honey-combs hanging on trees with countless bees busily engaged in collecting honey and hosts of angels busy day and night in milking these cows and getting honey and pouring them continuously into streams to keep them running? Are these ideas in keeping with the teachings of the verses which tell us that this world is a stranger to the blessings of the next world? Will these things illumine the soul or increase the knowledge of the Lord or afford spiritual food as the heavenly blessings are designed to do? It is, no doubt, true that these blessings are represented as material things, but we are also told that their source is spirituality and righteousness.

The following verse, which may ordinarily be misunderstood, is far from describing the heavenly blessings as being identical with the worldly things:

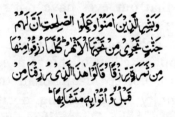

"And give good news to those who believe and do good deeds, that for them are Gardens in which rivers flow. Whenever they are given

a portion of the fruit thereof, they will say:
This is what was given to us before; and
they are given the like of it ... " — 2 : 25.

Now the context clearly shows that the fruits
which the righteous are said to have tasted here
do, by no means, signify the fruits of trees or the
things of this world. The verse in fact tells
us that those who believe and do good works
prepare a paradise with their own hands for
themselves, with their faith for trees and their
good deeds for fruits. It is of the fruits of this
garden that they are spiritually made to taste here
and of the fruits of the same will they eat in the
next life; only the spiritual fruits of this life will
be transformed into palpable and more delicious
fruits in the next life. But, as they will have
already tasted of them spiritually in this life,
they will be able to identify the fruits of that life
with those of this and, witnessing the close
resemblance between the two, will cry out : "these
are the fruits which were indeed given to us
in the former life."

Nature of next life

The verse quoted above tells us in plain words
that those who spiritually taste of the love of God
in this world will be physically sustained by the
same food in the next life. The blessings of the
next life will recall to their minds the spiritual

blessings of the love of God which they tasted in this life, and they will remember the time when in seclusion and at the dead of night, alone and in silence, they found their sweet enjoyment in the remembrance of the Lord.

If it be objected that the words of this verse contradict the saying of the Prophet which describes the blessings of heavenly life as unseen by worldly eyes, unheard of by human ears and inconceivable by the mind of man, the answer is that the contradiction exists only when we take the words "these are the fruits which were given us in our former life" as indicating temporal blessings, enjoyable in this life by all men whether good or bad. But if the "fruits" spoken of here be understood to mean the fruits of good works, the spiritual blessings which the good enjoy in this very life, there is no contradiction. Whatever the good men enjoy spiritually in this life are really blessings, not of this but of the next life and are granted to them as a specimen of the bliss that is in store for them in the next life in order to increase their yearning for it.

It should further be remembered that the righteous man is not of this world and hence he is hated down here. He is of heaven and is granted celestial blessings just as the worldly ones are granted the dainties of this world. The blessings which are granted him are really hidden from the eyes, the ears and the hearts of men and they are quite strangers to them. But the person whose life in this world has been transformed so that he tastes spiritually the cup which he shall actually quaff in the next world, shall truly utter the words : "these are the fruits which were given us formerly." However, he shall at the same time be perfectly aware that those blessings were quite unknown to the world, and as he too was in this world — though not of this world — so he also shall bear witness that his physical eye never saw such blessings, nor his ear ever heard of them, nor his mind ever conceived of them in the world. But in his second life, after his regeneration, he did witness specimens of these things but this was only when, all his lower connections having been cut asunder, higher ones were established with the next world.

The following verses will show how the Holy Quran has repeatedly asserted that the life after death is not a new life but only an image and a manifestation of the present one:

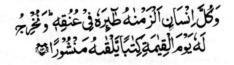

"And We have made every man's actions to cling to his neck, and We shall bring forth to

him on the day of Resurrection a book which
he will find wide open ... "1 — 17 : 13.

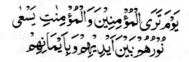

"On that day thou wilt see the faithful men and
the faithful women, their light gleaming before
them and on their right hands ... "2 — 57 : 12.

$$ \text{ٱلْهٰكُمُ ٱلتَّكَاثُرُ ۝ حَتّٰى زُرْتُمُ ٱلْمَقَابِرَ ۝ كَلَّا سَوْفَ} $$

"Abundance diverts you, until you come to the
graves. Nay, you will soon know, nay, again,
you will soon know. Nay, would that you knew
with a certain knowledge ! You will certainly

---

1. The Arabic word *ṭair*, used in this verse, literally means a "bird" and
is here used metaphorically to signify the actions of men; for every action,
whether good or bad, takes flight like a bird. The bliss or burden which
a person feels in the performance of an act vanishes but it leaves its impression upon the heart. The Quran has disclosed the important principle
that every act makes a mysterious impression upon the heart. Every
action of a man is in fact followed by an action of God which imprints its
good or bad effect not only upon the hearts but also upon the hands, the
feet, the ears, the eyes, etc., of the doer. This book which, hidden·from
the human eye, is being prepared, recording every action in this life,
shall show itself clearly in the next.

2. This verse refers to the heavenly life, while the verses which follow
(102: 1-8) relate to the wicked people.

see hell; then you will see it with certainty of
sight; then on that day you shall certainly be
questioned about the boons " [1] — 102 : 1-8.

It may be recalled here that the Holy Quran
has described three worlds of three different states
of man's life :

World of earning

The first is the present one, called the "world
of earning and of the first creation." It is here
that man earns a reward for the good or bad
deeds he does. Although there are stages of
advancement of the good after Resurrection, yet
that advancement is granted simply by the grace
of the Beneficent and does not depend upon
human efforts.

Intermediate state

The second is termed *barzakh*. The word
originally means any "intermediate state". It

---

1. God has here described three stages of certainty: *'ilm al-yaqin*
(certainty by inference), *'ain al-yaqin* (certainty by sight), and *haq al-yaqin*
(certainty by realization). A homely illustration would perhaps make
the subject easily comprehensible. If a person sees a column of smoke
from a distance, he readily concludes the existence of fire there, as nothing
else can give rise to smoke. He thus obtains a certainty by inference with
regard to the presence of fire, which is called the "certainty by knowledge"
in the verses quoted above. But, if he walks on to the place from which
the smoke rises and actually sees the flames, he obtains a knowledge with
the eye, which is "certainty by sight". To realize the truth of certainty,
he must thrust his hand into it and the certainty he thus attains to is
"certainty by realization". These are also the states of human knowledge
with regard to hell. The knowledge of certainty can be had in this world
by those who will, but in the interval between death and resurrection a
man sees hell with the eye of certainty, while at the day of resurrection he
shall realize the truth of the certainty by himself entering into hell.

has been thus called because this world falls
between the present life and Resurrection. But
this word has from time immemorial been applied
to an intermediate state and thus the word itself
is a standing witness to the intermediate state
between death and after-life.[1]

The state of *barzakh* is that in which the soul
leaves the mortal body, and the perishable remains
are decomposed. The body is thrown into a pit
and the soul also is, as it were, thrown down into
a pit as is indicated by the word, because it loses
the power to do good or bad deeds along with
its loss of control over the body. It is evident
that a good state of the soul is dependent upon the
soundness of the body. A shock communicated
to a particular part of the brain causes a loss of
memory, while an injury to another part is certain
to injure the reasoning faculty and may even
destroy consciousness. Similarly, a convulsion
of the brain muscles or a hemorrhage or morbidity
of the brain may, by causing obstruction, lead
to insensibility, epilepsy or cerebral apoplexy.

---

1. *Barzakh* is a word of Arabic origin and is a compound of *bar* and *zakh*,
and literally means that "the period of earning merit or demerit by deeds is
over". I might add here that I have shown in my book *Minān al-Raḥmān*
that the words of Arabic language are the words of God, and that it is the
only language which can claim to be Divine, the fountain from which all
sorts of knowledge flow, the mother of all languages and the first as well
as the last medium of Divine revelation. It is first because Arabic
was the Word of God, which had at last been revealed to the world, from
which men learned to make their own languages, and the last because
the last Divine Book (the Quran) is also in Arabic.

Experience, therefore, establishes the fact beyond all reasonable doubt that with all its connections severed from the body, the soul can serve no purpose. It is idle to assert that the human soul can, at any time, enjoy a bliss without having any connection with the body. It may please us as an interesting tale, but reason and experience lend no support to it. We can hardly imagine the soul to be in a perfect condition when all its connections with the body are cut off, in the face of our daily experience that the slightest derangement of the physical system interrupts the functions of the soul as well. Do we not witness that when a person becomes decrepit with old age, the soul also is enfeebled and age often steals away the whole store of its knowledge? With reference to the decrepitude of old age, the Quran says :

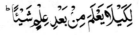

"(A man lives to such an old age) that, after knowledge, he knows nothing " — 22 : 5.

These observations should be sufficient to demonstrate that the soul is nothing unless it has its connection with a body. Had it any value apart from the body, the action of an All-Wise Being in uniting the soul with a short-lived body would have been quite meaningless. Moreover, man is essentially a progressive animal, and the advancement which he aims at is by no means a limited one. Now, if the soul is unable to make any advancement in the brief life without the assistance of the body, how could it attain to the higher stages of advancement in the next life ?

Various arguments, therefore, prove conclusively that, according to the Islamic principles, the perfection of soul depends upon its permanent connection with a body. There is no doubt that, after death, this body of clay is separated from the soul but, then, in the *barzakh* every soul receives temporarily a new body to be in a position to taste of the reward or punishment of its deeds. This new body is not a body of clay but a bright or a dark body prepared from the actions of this life. It may appear as a mystery to some, but this much at least must be admitted that it is not unreasonable. The perfect being realizes the preparation of such a bright body even in this life. Ordinary human understanding may regard it as a mystery which is beyond human comprehension, but those who have a keen and bright spiritual sight will have no difficulty in realizing the truth of a bright or a dark body after death, prepared from actions in this life. In other words, the new body granted in the *barzakh* becomes the means of the reward of good or evil.[1]

---

1. I may state here that I have personal experience in this matter. Many a time, when fully awake, I have had visions in which I saw those

It must also be remembered in connection with this point that the Word of God has described those who walk in error and wickedness as dead and lifeless, while the good it calls living. The secret of it is that the means of life of those who are ignorant of the Lord, being simply eating, drinking or indulging in their bestial passions, are cut off along with their death. Of spiritual food they have no share and, therefore, their resurrection will only be for their punishment. We are told :

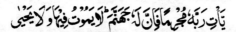

"Whoso comes guilty to his Lord, for him is hell.
He will neither die therein, nor live "— 20 : 74.

It may be added that the chosen ones of God do not die with their physical death, for they have their means of sustenance with them.

Resurrection

The third is the world of Resurrection. In this world, every soul, good or bad, virtuous or wicked, shall be given a visible body. The Day

---

who were dead. I have seen many an evildoer and a wicked person with a body quite dark and smoky. I have personal acquaintance with these matters and I assert it strongly that, as God has said, everyone is granted a body either transparent or dark. It is not necessary that unaided reason should be able to look into these mysteries. The eye sees things, but it is in vain to expect it to serve as an organ of taste. Similarly, the muscles of the tongue may be used for tasting things, but as organs of sight they are useless. In like manner, the deep secrets of the other world, upon which light is thrown only by visions, cannot be discovered by the help of reason. The Almighty has established certain laws in this world and particular means for the knowledge of particular things.

of Resurrection is the day of the complete
manifestation of the Lord's glory when everyone
will become perfectly aware of the existence of
God. On that day, every person will have an
open and complete reward of his actions. How
this can be brought about is not a matter to
wonder at, for the Creator is All-Powerful and
nothing is impossible with Him. Thus He says :

اَوَلَمۡ يَرَ الۡاِنۡسَانُ اَنَّا خَلَقۡنٰهُ مِنۡ نُّطۡفَةٍ فَاِذَا هُوَ خَصِيۡمٌ
مُّبِيۡنٌ ۞ وَضَرَبَ لَنَا مَثَلًا وَّنَسِىَ خَلۡقَهٗ ؕ قَالَ مَنۡ يُّحۡىِ الۡعِظَامَ
وَهِىَ رَمِيۡمٌ ۞ قُلۡ يُحۡيِيۡهَا الَّذِىۡۤ اَنۡشَاَهَاۤ اَوَّلَ مَرَّةٍ ؕ وَهُوَ بِكُلِّ
خَلۡقٍ عَلِيۡمٌ ۙ الَّذِىۡ جَعَلَ لَكُمۡ مِّنَ الشَّجَرِ الۡاَخۡضَرِ نَارًا فَاِذَاۤ
اَنۡتُمۡ مِّنۡهُ تُوۡقِدُوۡنَ ۞ اَوَلَيۡسَ الَّذِىۡ خَلَقَ السَّمٰوٰتِ وَالۡاَرۡضَ
بِقٰدِرٍ عَلٰۤى اَنۡ يَّخۡلُقَ مِثۡلَهُمۡ ؕ بَلٰى وَهُوَ الۡخَلّٰقُ الۡعَلِيۡمُ ۞ اِنَّمَاۤ
اَمۡرُهٗۤ اِذَاۤ اَرَادَ شَيۡئًا اَنۡ يَّقُوۡلَ لَهٗ كُنۡ فَيَكُوۡنُ ۞ فَسُبۡحٰنَ
الَّذِىۡ بِيَدِهٖ مَلَكُوۡتُ كُلِّ شَىۡءٍ وَّاِلَيۡهِ تُرۡجَعُوۡنَ ۞

"Does not man see that We have created him
from the small life-germ? Then lo! he is an
open disputant. And he strikes out a likeness
for Us and forgets his own creation. Says he:
Who will give life to the bones, when they are
rotten? Say: He will give life to them, Who
brought them into existence at first, and He is
Knower of all creation, Who produced fire for

you out of the green tree, so that with
it you kindle. Is not He Who created the
heavens and the earth able to create the like
of them? Yea! and He is the Creator
(of all), the Knower. His command, when
He intends anything, is only to say to it,
Be, and it is. So glory be to Him in Whose
hand is the Kingdom of all things! and to
Him you will be returned" — 36 : 77-83.

It is to be noted that in these verses the
Almighty tells us that with Him nothing is
impossible, for when He could create man out of
an insignificant thing at first, He cannot be
regarded as destitute of the power to bring
him to life a second time.

Reward and punishment

Before proceeding further, it seems necessary
to deal with an objection here. It might be
argued that when a long period of time must
elapse before the world of Resurrection is brought
in existence, the *barzakh*, where the souls of both
good and bad men must remain in the meanwhile,
is no better than a useless lock-up for souls. The
objection is based upon ignorance, for the *barzakh*
is as well a place of reward for good and evil as
the Resurrection itself. The Quran describes it as
a place where punishment and reward shall be
given though not so openly as after the Resurrection. It abounds with verses stating that a man

meets with his due immediately after his death. Thus speaking of a certain person, it says :

$$قِيْلَ ادْخُلِ الْجَنَّةَ$$

"It was said (to the man who believed in the Truth): Enter the Garden" — 36 : 26.

With reference to another person, the Holy Book says the following:

$$فَرَآهُ فِيْ سَوَآءِ الْجَحِيْمِ$$

"Then he looked down and saw him (his friend) in the midst of hell" [1] — 37 : 55.

Punishment and reward are thus bestowed immediately after death, and those whose proper place is hell are brought to hell, while those who deserve paradise are brought to paradise. But the Day of Resurrection is the day of the manifestation of the highest glory of God which His transcendent wisdom has ordained should at last be brought about. The Lord created man that He might be accepted as the Creator : He will destroy all that He may be recognized as a Vanquisher of all, and, finally, He will give a perfect life to all and assemble them that He may be recognized as the All-Powerful Being.

---

1. A good man had an unbelieving friend in this life and when they both died, the good man, anxious to know the state of his friend, was shown that he was in the midst of hell.

Value of spiritual facts

The second point of importance, which the Quran has described with reference to the life to come, is that the spiritual facts of this life shall be represented in the next as embodiment :

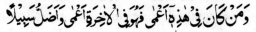

"And whoever is blind in this (world) he will be blind in the Hereafter, and further away from the (right) path"[1] — 17 : 72.

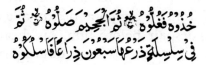

"Seize him, then fetter him, then cast him into the burning Fire, then insert him in a chain the length of which is seventy cubits"[2] — 69: 30-32.

In these verses, the spiritual torture of this world has been represented as a physical punishment in the next. The chain to be put round the neck, for instance, represents the desires of

---

1. In other words, the spiritual blindness of this world shall become apparent and shall be seen as actual blindness in the next.

2. The thrusting into a chain of the length of seventy cubits reveals the same secret. The limit of age may, as a general rule, be fixed at seventy. The wicked person would sometimes even enjoy seventy years excluding the periods of childhood and decrepitude. These seventy years during which he could work with honesty, wisdom and zeal, he wastes away only in the entanglements of the world and in following his own sensual passions. He does not try to free himself from the chain of desires and, therefore, in the next world, this chain, which he indulged in for seventy years, will be embodied into a chain seventy cubits long, every cubit representing a year, in which he will be fettered.

this world which keep a man with his head bent upon the earth, and it is these desires that shall assume the shape of a chain. Similarly, the entanglements of this world shall be seen as chains on the feet. The heart-burning of this world shall likewise be clearly seen as flames of burning fire. The wicked one has, in fact, in this very world, within himself, a hell of the passions and inextinguishable desires of this world and feels the burning of that hell in the frustrations he meets with. When, therefore, he will be cast farther off from his temporal desires and will see an everlasting despair before him, his heart burning and bitter sighs for his dear desires will assume the shape of burning fire. The Holy Book says :

وَحِيلَ بَيْنَهُمْ وَبَيْنَ مَا يَشْتَهُونَ

"And a barrier is placed between them and
that which they desire..." — 34 : 54.

It should, therefore, be remembered that the punishment which overtakes a man is one prepared by his own hands, and his own evil deeds become the source of his torture. This law is elsewhere expressed in the following words :

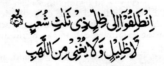

"(O ye wicked ones) walk on to the shadow,

having three branches, neither cool, nor
availing against the flame " [1] — 77 : 30-31.

To declare the same law, the Almighty says
of those who are in paradise :

يَوْمَ تَرَى الْمُؤْمِنِينَ وَالْمُؤْمِنَاتِ يَسْعَى
نُورُهُمْ بَيْنَ أَيْدِيهِمْ وَبِأَيْمَانِهِمْ

"On that day thou wilt see the faithful men and
the faithful women, their light gleaming before
them and on their right hands." — 57 : 12.

يَوْمَ تَبْيَضُّ وُجُوهٌ وَتَسْوَدُّ وُجُوهٌ

"On the day when (some) faces turn white
and (some) faces turn black . . ." — 3 : 105.

مَثَلُ الْجَنَّةِ الَّتِي وُعِدَ الْمُتَّقُونَ فِيهَا أَنْهَارٌ مِّن مَّاءٍ غَيْرِ
آسِنٍ وَأَنْهَارٌ مِّن لَّبَنٍ لَّمْ يَتَغَيَّرْ طَعْمُهُ وَأَنْهَارٌ مِّن
خَمْرٍ لَّذَّةٍ لِّلشَّارِبِينَ وَأَنْهَارٌ مِّنْ عَسَلٍ مُّصَفًّى

"A parable of the Garden which the dutiful (to
Allāh) are promised: Therein are rivers of
water not altering for the worse, and rivers
of milk whereof the taste changes not, and
rivers of wine delicious to the drinkets, and
rivers of honey clarified . . . " — 47 : 15.

---

1. The three branches spoken of here represent bestiality, savageness and
infatuation which, remaining unmodified, lead to transgressions and evil
deeds. These three will appear on the Day of Judgment as three branches
without any leaves and, therefore, availing nothing against heat.

From this verse, it appears clearly that the promised paradise is only a representation of boundless oceans of all these things. The water of life which the righteous man drinks spiritually in this world shall there appear manifestly as a river; the spiritual milk with which he remains in a blissful state in this world shall assume the shape of a river flowing with wine, and the honey of the sweetness of faith, which he spiritually tastes here, will flow in paradise in palpable rivers. The spiritual state of every person will, on that day, become visible to all in his gardens and rivers, and God also will reveal Himself to the righteous in His full glory on that day. In short, the spiritual states will no more remain hidden but will manifest themselves palpably.

Infinite progress

The third point of importance that the Holy Quran has described in connection with the life after death is that the progress that can be made in that life is infinite :

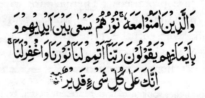

"And those who believe with him (the Prophet), their light will gleam before them and on their

right hands — they will say: Our Lord, make
perfect for us our light, and grant us protection!
Lo! Thou art Able to do all things " — 66 : 8.

This unceasing desire for perfection shows
clearly that progress in paradise will be endless.
For, when they will have attained one excellence
they will not stop there but, seeing a higher
stage of excellence, will consider that to
which they will have attained as imperfect
and will, therefore, desire the attainment of the
higher excellence. When they will have attained
to this, they will yet see another higher excellence
and thus they will continue to pray for the attainment of higher and higher excellences. This
ceaseless desire for perfection shows that they
will be endlessly attaining to excellences: the
righteous will go on making progress and will
never recede a step nor shall they ever be deprived
of those blessings.[1]

---

1. The question may arise here as to the seeking of *maghfirat* after entry
into paradise and obtaining God's pardon. Such a question is, however,
based upon ignorance of the actual meaning of *maghfirat* and *istighfár*.
Maghfirat really means "suppression of a defective state". The righteous
will be continually praying to the Lord for the attainment of perfection
and complete immersion in light. They will be ever ascending upwards
and will regard every state as defective in comparison with a higher one to
which they will aspire and will, therefore, pray God to suppress the defective
state that they may be able to get to the higher one. Their desire for
maghfirat will, therefore, be endless because the progress which they will
have to make will also be endless. We can clearly see from this that the
true significance of the word *istighfár* and also that the desire of it is really
the pride of man, because it is the only thing which leads him on to the
highest excellences which a man can possess.

In short, heaven and hell, according to the Quran, are images and representations of a man's own spiritual life in this world. They are not new material worlds which come from outside. It is true that they will be visible and palpable, call them material, if you will, but they are only embodiments of the spiritual facts of this life. We call them material not in the sense that there will be trees planted in the paradisical fields just like those that are planted here below and that there will be brimstone and sulphur in hell, but in the sense that we shall there find the embodiments of the spiritual facts of this life. Heaven and hell, according to Islamic belief, are the images of the actions which we perform down here.

OBJECT OF MAN'S EXISTENCE

> "And strive hard in Allāh's way with
> your wealth and your lives . . . " — 9 : 41.

The third question relates to the objects of man's
life here below, and the means by which those
objects may be attained.

Real object

It is needless to say that different men have,
on account of their superficial views on narrow-
mindedness, set before themselves different objects
generally limited to a gratification of low desires
and pleasures of this world. But the Almighty
has declared a higher aim of man's existence :

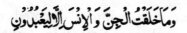

> "And I have not created the jinn and the men
> except that they should serve Me" — 51: 56.

The real object of man's life according to the Quran is, therefore, a true knowledge and worship of God and a total resignation to His will so that whatever is said or done is for His sake only. One thing, at least, is plain: man has no choice in the matter of fixing the aim of life. He is a creature, and the Creator, Who has brought him into existence and bestowed upon him higher and more excellent faculties than upon other animals, has also assigned an object to his existence. A man may or may not understand it, or a hundred different motives may hold him back from it, but the truth is that the grand aim of man's life consists in knowing and worshiping God and living for His sake. The Lord says:

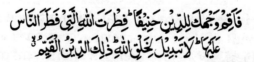

"Lo! religion with Allāh is Islām ... " — 3 : 18.

إِنَّ الدِّينَ عِنْدَ اللهِ الْإِسْلَامُ

فَأَقِمْ وَجْهَكَ لِلدِّينِ حَنِيفًا ۚ فِطْرَتَ اللهِ الَّتِي فَطَرَ النَّاسَ عَلَيْهَا ۚ لَا تَبْدِيلَ لِخَلْقِ اللهِ ۚ ذَلِكَ الدِّينُ الْقَيِّمُ

"So set thy face for religion, being upright, the nature made by Allāh in which He has created men. There is no altering Allāh's creation. That is the right religion ... " — 30 : 30.

We cannot enter into a detailed commentary on these verses here. Something has already been said in answer to the third part of the first question regarding this point. We may, however, add a few remarks upon the wonderful aptitude of the faculties of man for Islam.

Endowments

The external and internal endowments of human nature give us clearly to understand that the highest object of their creation is the love and worship of God. True happiness, which is generally admitted to be the goal of life, is not attainable through the diverse pursuits which men follow but only through the Divine Being. Not all the felicities of this world can afford relief from the gnawing grief which attends a man's last moments upon this earth. The greatest king, the wisest philosopher, the highest official or the richest merchant does not possess contentment of mind, and departs from this world a prey to poignant regret. His heart upbraids him for his absorption in worldly cares and his conscience judges him guilty of the employment of unfair means to attain success in his worldly affairs.

Let us consider the question in an other light. In the case of the lower animals, we see that their faculties are so made as to render them unable to serve a purpose higher than a particular one and they cannot go beyond a certain limit. This leads us to the conclusion that the highest limit which the faculties of a particular animal can reach is also the highest aim of its creation. A bullock, for instance, may be used to furrow the land or draw water or for loading, but with its present faculties it can serve no higher purpose. This is, therefore, also the aim of its existence.

Judging man in the same manner, we find that, of all the faculties which nature has bestowed upon him, the highest is that which awakens him to a search for God and encourages him to the noble aspiration of losing his own self in the love of the Beneficent and completely submitting himself to His will. In the requirements of his physical nature, the lower animals are on a level with him. In art, some animals display more skill than human beings. The bee produces honey from the juice of many flowers with such exquisite skill that man has failed to achieve anything like it. The perfection of man, therefore, does not consist in these matters but in something else. It consists in the excellence of his spirituality in his union with God. The true object of his life in this world is that the window of his heart should be opened towards the Creator.

Means of attainment

We are now in a position to answer the second part of the question: how this object can possibly be attained?

The first means towards the attainment of this end is that, in the recognition of the Lord, a man should tread upon the right path and have his faith in the true and living God. The goal can never be reached by the man who takes the first step in the wrong direction and looks upon some stone or creature or an element of nature as his deity. The true Master assists those who seek Him, but a dead deity cannot assist its dead worshippers. The Almighty has well illustrated this in the following parable:

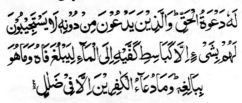

"To Him (Allāh) is due the true prayer. And those to whom they pray besides Him give them no answer, but (they are) like he who stretches forth his two hands towards water that it may reach his mouth, but it will not reach it. And the prayer of the disbelievers is only wasted" — 13 : 14.

The second means to attain the true object of life consists in being informed of the perfect beauty which the Benefactor possesses. Beauty naturally attracts the heart and incites love. The beauty of God consists in His unity, His majesty, His grandeur and His other lofty attributes. The

Holy Quran draws attention to this point in
the following words :

قُلْ هُوَ اللّٰهُ اَحَدٌ ۞ اَللّٰهُ الصَّمَدُ ۞ لَمْ يَلِدْ هُ وَلَمْ
يُولَدْ ۞ وَلَمْ يَكُنْ لَّهُ كُفُوًا اَحَدٌ ۞

"Say: He, Allāh, is One. Allāh is He on
Whom all depend. He begets not, nor is He
begotten; and none is like Him"[1] — 112: 1-4.

The third means of reaching the goal consists
in realizing the immense goodness of the Lord.
Beauty and kindness are the only two incentives to
love. The attributes of God in this respect are
described in the opening chapter of the Quran:

اَلْحَمْدُ لِلّٰهِ رَبِّ الْعَلَمِينَ ۞ الرَّحْمٰنِ
الرَّحِيْمِ ۞ مٰلِكِ يَوْمِ الدِّيْنِ ۞

"Praise be to Allāh, the Lord of the
worlds, the Beneficent, the Merciful, Master
of the day of Requital ... " — 1 : 2-4.

It is plain that the Divine goodness could not
be perfect unless the Creator first brought everything into existence from nothing and then gave
it sustenance under all circumstances and Himself

---

1. The Quran teems with verses declaring the omnipotence, majesty
and glory of the Almighty. It presents a God Who attracts the heart on
account of His beauty and majesty, and rejects the dead, weak, unmerciful
and powerless gods of false religions.

supported it in its weakness. All aspects of His mercy should come into play for His creatures, and His kindness should have no limits set to it. To this perfect goodness, the Holy Book says:

وَإِن تَعُدُّوا نِعْمَتَ اللّٰهِ لَا تُحْصُوهَا

"And if you count Allāh's favours, you will not be able to number them..." — 14 : 34.

The fourth means for the desired end is prayer. The Lord of the worlds says:

ادْعُونِي أَسْتَجِبْ لَكُمْ

"Pray to Me, I will answer you..."—40 : 60.

It may be noted that frequent stress has been laid upon this point in the Quran, because man can reach the Merciful only with Divine assistance.

The fifth means is to seek God by spending one's substance and faculties, and sacrificing one's life and applying one's wisdom in His way:

وَجَاهِدُوا بِأَمْوَالِكُمْ وَأَنْفُسِكُمْ فِي سَبِيلِ اللّٰهِ

"And strive hard in Allāh's way with your wealth and your lives..." — 9 : 41.

وَمِمَّا رَزَقْنَاهُمْ يُنْفِقُونَ

"(This Book is a guide to those who) spend out

of what We have given them..." — 2 : 3.

والَّذِينَ جَاهَدُوا فِينَا لَنَهْدِيَنَّهُمْ سُبُلَنَا

"And those who strive hard for Us, We shall surely guide them in Our ways..." — 29:69.

The sixth means by which a person may safely attain to the goal is perseverance, that is, he should be indefatigable in the way in which he walks and unswerving under the hardest trial:

"(As for) those who say, Our Lord is Allāh, then continue in the right way, the angels descend upon them, saying: Fear not, nor be grieved, and receive good news of the Garden which you were promised. We are your friends in this world's life and in the Hereafter..."—41:30-31.

In these verses, we are told that perseverance in faith brings about the pleasure of God. It is true, as the Arabic proverb goes, that "perseverance is more than a miracle." The highest degree of perseverance is called forth when adversities encompass a man all around, when he is threatened with loss of life, property and honour in the Divine path, and whatever is consoling or comforting forsakes him so much so that the Lord tries him even by closing the door of visions and revelations for a time.

It is when a man is surrounded by these dreary sights and the last ray of hope disappears that perseverance must be shown. Under such ills and sufferings a man must show firmness, not swerve from the line, hold on through fire and flood, be willing to suffer every disgrace, wait for no succour or support, not even seek any good tidings from on High and, in spite of his helplessness and the absence of all comfort, he must stand up firmly, submitting himself to the heavenly will without wringing his hands or beating his breast.

This is the true perseverance which reveals the glorious face of God. It is this noble quality which the apostles, the righteous and the faithful still exhale. Referring to this, the Lord of the worlds directs the believers to pray to Him in the following words:

اِهْدِنَا الصِّرَاطَ الْمُسْتَقِيمَ ۞

"Guide us on the right path" — 1 : 6.

صِرَاطَ الَّذِينَ اَنْعَمْتَ عَلَيْهِمْ

"The path of those (believers) upon whom

Thou hast bestowed (Thy) favours " — 1 : 7.

رَبَّنَاۤ أَفْرِغْ عَلَيْنَا صَبْرًا وَتَوَفَّنَا مُسْلِمِينَ

"Our Lord, pour out on us patience and cause
us to die in submission (to Thee) ! "— 7 : 126.

It should be noted that in afflictions and
trials, the Merciful causes a light to descend upon
the hearts of His faithful servants, strengthened
with which they meet all trials with calmness and
dignity and, on acconnt of the sweetness of their
faith, kiss the chains they are bound with for
walking in the right path. When the righteous
servants are under hard trials and sufferings and
see death face to face, they do not supplicate their
Creator to remove their sufferings. They know
that to pray to Him to remove the cup of their
hard lot is opposing His will and not in accordance
with total resignation to it. The true lover does
not recede but takes a forward step when he sees
ills and adversities and, looking upon his own life
as a very insignificant thing, willingly submits
himself to the will of heaven and is prepared to
meet the worst. Of such people, the Lord says:

وَمِنَ النَّاسِ مَنْ يَشْرِى نَفْسَهُ ابْتِغَاءَ
مَرْضَاتِ اللهِ وَاللهُ رَءُوفٌ بِالْعِبَادِ

"And of men is he who sells himself to seek

the pleasure of Allāh. And Allāh is (indeed) Compassionate to the servants " — 2 : 207.

In short, this is the essence of the constancy which leads to the Divine Being.

The seventh means to attain the object is to keep company with the righteous and to imitate their perfect example. This underlines the need of the appearance of prophets.

Man is naturally inclined to imitate a model and feels the need of it. A perfect model infuses life into a person and invigorates him to act upon the principles of righteousness, while he who does not imitate a perfect model gradually loses all eagerness to do good and ultimately falls into error. To this end, the Quran says:

وَكُوْنُوْا مَعَ الصّٰدِقِيْنَ

"(O believers), be with the truthful" — 9 : 119.

The eighth means is true visions and revelations from God. As the path which leads to the Creator is a secret and mysterious one, and is full of difficulties and dangers, the spiritual wayfarer may depart from the right course or despair of attaining the goal. The Divine grace, therefore, continues to encourage and strengthen him in his spiritual journey, gives him consolation in moments of grief and animates him with a still more zealous desire to pursue his journey eagerly.

Such is the Divine law with the wayfarers of His path that He continues to cheer their hearts with His word and to reveal to them that He is with them ! Thus strengthened, they undertake this journey with great vigour. The Holy Book says :

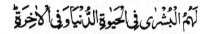

"For them (the believers) is good news in this world's life and in the Hereafter " — 10 : 64.

It may be added that the Quran has described numerous other ways which assist us in reaching the goal of life, but we cannot describe them here for want of space.

RESULTS PRODUCED BY ACTIONS

"And We have made every man's action to cling to his neck, and We shall bring forth to him on the day of Resurrection a book which he will find wide open . . . " — 17: 13.

How does a true and perfect Law, revealed by God, practically operate upon the heart of man is the fourth question which will be briefly considered. It may be recalled that this has been partly discussed while dealing with the first question.

Perfect man

A perfect Divine Law enables a man to rise from the lowest depths of ignorance to the highest pinnacles of light and knowledge ; it turns the savage into a man, the man into a highly moral being and, last of all, transforms his morality into spirituality and godliness.

The injunctions of the Law have, moreover, the effect of regulating a man's relations with his fellow-beings and of increasing his sympathy for them. By its aid, he begins gradually to see and know their rights and, in his dealings with them, he applies his attributes of justice, goodness and sympathy on the proper occasion. He freely gives to each, according to his desert, a share of his knowledge, substance, comforts, and other blessings which the Merciful has granted him. Like the sun, he sheds his lustre over all and, like the moon, transmits to others the light which he borrows from the great and original source of light. He brightens like the day and shows the ways of truth and virtue and again, like the night, he draws the veil over the faults and misdeeds of others, and affords rest to the tired and weary. Like the heavens, he takes every distressed one under his shelter and revives the lifeless earth with salubrious rain and, like the earth, he submits himself in all humility and lowliness to be trampled under the feet of others as a trial for them and furnishes them with many kinds of spiritual fruits.

The effect of walking in obedience to the ordinances of a perfect Law, therefore, is that a man is able to perform his duty towards God and man in a fitting and creditable manner. He is totally resigned to the Divine will and completely engaged in the service of humanity. Such is the transformation which obedience to the Law brings about in man in this life.

In the next life, the spiritual union with the Creator will find a clearer manifestation in being afforded the sight of the Almighty and the services of His creatures — which one has done simply out of His love and to which faith and the desire of good deeds are the only incentives — will be symbolized into the trees and the rivers of paradise. The following verses of the Holy Book may be quoted in this connection:

وَالشَّمْسِ وَضُحَاهَا ۞ وَالْقَمَرِ إِذَا تَلَاهَا ۞ وَالنَّهَارِ إِذَا جَلَّاهَا ۞
وَالَّيْلِ إِذَا يَغْشَاهَا ۞ وَالسَّمَاءِ وَمَا بَنَاهَا ۞ وَالْأَرْضِ وَمَا
طَحَاهَا ۞ وَنَفْسٍ وَمَا سَوَّاهَا ۞ فَأَلْهَمَهَا فُجُورَهَا وَتَقْوَاهَا ۞
قَدْ أَفْلَحَ مَنْ زَكَّاهَا ۞ وَقَدْ خَابَ مَنْ دَسَّاهَا ۞
كَذَّبَتْ ثَمُودُ بِطَغْوَاهَا ۞ إِذِ انْبَعَثَ أَشْقَاهَا ۞ فَقَالَ لَهُمْ
رَسُولُ اللَّهِ نَاقَةَ اللَّهِ وَسُقْيَاهَا ۞ فَكَذَّبُوهُ فَعَقَرُوهَا فَدَمْدَمَ
عَلَيْهِمْ رَبُّهُمْ بِذَنْبِهِمْ فَسَوَّاهَا ۞ وَلَا يَخَافُ عُقْبَاهَا

"By the sun and his brightness![1] And the moon when she borrows light from him ! And the day when it exposes it to view ! And the night when it draws a veil over it ! And the heaven and its make! And the earth and its extension!

1. This is to show that the spiritual light of Prophet Muḥammad will brighten as time passes on — Publisher.

And the soul and its perfection !—So He reveals
to it its way of evil and its way of good;[1] he is
indeed successful who causes it to grow, and he
indeed fails who buries it. Thamūd rejected
(the truth) in their inordinacy, when the basest
of them broke forth with mischief—So Allāh's
messenger said to them: (Leave alone) Allāh's
she-camel, and (give) her (to) drink. But they
called him a liar and slaughtered her. So
their Lord destroyed them for their sin
and levelled them (with the ground); and He
fears not its consequence "[2] — 91 : 1-15.

The wretched who does not purify his soul
really wounds the camel of God and deprives her
of the water of his fountain. This alludes to the
fact that the spirit of man is the camel of God,
which he rides upon, that is, the heart of man is
the throne of the manifestation of the Creator's
glories, and the water which is the source of the
life of that camel is the love and knowledge of the
Almighty. As to the consequences of Thamūd's

1. The verse is a fitting sequel to the statement made in the previous
verse as regards the prefection of soul, as it points out the way to
perfection: through Divine inspiration.

2. The promise of being saved from death is an allusion to the eternal
life which will be granted to the perfect one hereafter. This shows that
a virtuous course of life in obedience to the commandments of the Law
leads to eternal life hereafter for which the sight of God will serve as a
sustenance. Then we are told that: "He is undone and must despair
of his life, who has corrupted his soul (and departs from this world having
led an impure life and without having attained the excellences for which
the Lord had granted him the respective faculties)", and warns by way
of illustration: "The fate of that wretched will be the same as that of
Thamūd who hamstrung the camel which was called the 'Camel of
God' and did not allow her to drink from their fountain."

rejection, we are told that "when they wounded the camel and hindered her from drinking, they were destroyed and God cared neither for their youngs nor for their widows." Such is the fate of every person who hurts the camel of his spirit, does not care for its perfection, and withholds it from the water of life !

Divine oaths

God's swearing by His creatures is a method adopted by the Quran at which the opponents of Islam have too often stumbled, but their objections are due to lack of reflection. The oaths of the Book have underlying in them secrets of a very deep nature. The critics, being unable to comprehend them, have taken them for a flaw. In order to understand this subject fully, we must consider the meaning of swearing.

In ordinary transactions or legal proceedings, when a person takes an oath, his object is simply to supply the deficiency of insufficient testimony. He really calls the Lord to witness when there is no other witness in the case; for the Almighty is the Knower of secrets and the best Witness in every case. The manner in which he intends God to bear testimony is by His action, viz., that the truth of his assertion shall be confirmed if the Almighty does not send down His punishment upon him after the oath, as a mark of His displeasure which must follow a false oath. It is for this reason, too, that a man is forbidden to swear by the name of any creature, for the latter has no power either to know his secrets or to punish him for a false oath.

The object and meaning of Divine oaths must, however, be distinguished from those of mortals. Divine laws reveal a twofold nature of the works of God: obvious and inferential. The former are easily comprehensible, and regarding them very few or no differences exist; but in the comprehension of the latter there is a liability of error and much difference of opinion. In the form of oath, the Supreme Being has called attention to what may be inferred from what is obvious.

To take the oaths, mentioned in the verses quoted above, we see that the sun and the moon, day and night, heaven and earth belong to the former class and their properties are known to all. But the same properties as found in the soul of man are not obvious. To lead to an inference of the existence of these properties in the spirit of man, the Creator has called to witness His obvious works. The brief oaths may thus be unfolded into a chain of reasoning. The hidden excellences possessed by the soul of man are inferred from the manifest working of the sun and the moon... Man is but a miniature universe, and in his soul is represented on a small scale all that exists in the external universe. By creating man, the Lord has, as it were, enclosed in a nutshell the various forces existing in the world.

Now it is plain that the great bodies of the universe, for instance, have certain properties and forces which they employ in the service of God's creatures. It is, therefore, contrary to all reason to assert that man, who is above them all and greater than all of them, should be destitute of benefitting the rest of creation like them. Like the sun, he possesses a light — the light of wisdom and knowledge — with which he can enlighten the world. Like the moon, he borrows a light from the Most High, the original source of light, the light of vision, inspiration and revelation, which he transmits to those who are yet in the dark and have not attained to the perfection of humanity. It is sheer ignorance, then, to assert that prophethood is a pretence and that a message from on High, Divine Law and heavenly Books are mere impostures to achieve some private end.

Consider again how daylight renders manifest every path and reveals its ups and downs. The perfect man is the day of spiritual light. His appearance brings the different paths into view and points out the right from the wrong, for he is the bright day of truth and virtue. We observe, in like manner, that the night affords rest to the tired and the weary. The ever-spent labourer of the day welcomes the night and goes to rest, relieved of the day's toil.

Similarly, the perfect man comes to give rest to the world and to lighten the burden of men. With his inspirations and revelations from the source of wisdom and knowledge, he pours balm into the souls of all understanding men. Great truths, which wise people could not have discovered despite hard work, are disclosed with ease through the inspired one. Revelation, moreover, assists reason and covers up its faults, for it conceals its failings from the world. The wise man reforms himself and corrects his errors by the guidance and light of revelation and thus, with its aid, he saves himself from public exposure. This is the reason why a Greek philosopher, Plato, committed himself to the unwise act of making an offering to an idol, while no such act is recorded of any Muslim philosopher, because the latter had the perfect revelation of Prophet Muḥammad for the guidance of reason. It will thus be understood why the Almighty has called attention to the covering of night in the form of an oath.

It is, moreover, clear that the perfect servants of the Lord take every distressed and fatigued person under their shelter like heaven. The prophets especially benefit the world with the showers of their blessings and favours as heaven does with the showers of rain. They, likewise, possess the properties of the earth, and from their purified souls various sorts of trees of knowledge and truth grow up in abundance and, with their flowers and fruits, they bless the world. Thus the laws which we read in the open book of nature are a witness to the hidden laws and their testimony has been described in the form of oaths in the verses quoted above. How excellent is the wisdom displayed in the Divine Word! And this is the Word which has been proclaimed through the mouth of an unlettered son of the desert. Had it not been the wise Word of God, the educated sons of the wordly-wise would not thus have been driven to their wit's end and, failing at last to realize the true sense with their imperfect reason, have objected to these passages where treasures of wisdom lay concealed.

Thus we see that when worldly wisdom fails to discover the true meaning of words, which are afterwards shown to be pregnant with meaning, this constitutes a strong testimony to the superhuman origin of the words. Such has been the case with regard to the oaths of the Quran which were considered as weak and vulnerable points, but, now when the mystery has been solved and light has been thrown upon their true significance, all sensible persons should derive pleasure from reflecting on this subject.

Heavenly and earthly waters

The Holy Book has also resorted to the form of an oath in another place when describing the need and truth of revelation by appealing to the laws of Nature:

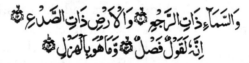

"By the cloud giving rain, and the earth opening (with herbage)! Surely it is a decisive word, and it is not a joke" — 86 : 11-14.

Here, the Almighty calls attention to His manifest law in the form of an oath as testimony for the truth of the revelation of the Quran. It is plainly seen in the laws of Nature that rain comes down from heaven in time of need. The greenness and verdure of the earth depend upon heavenly rain. If it ceases for a time, the water in the upper strata of the earth gradually dries up. Thus we perceive that there is a connection between the heavenly and the earthly waters. Revelation stands in the same relation to human reason as heavenly water does to the earthly water. As with the cessation of heavenly water earthly water begins gradually to dry up, so also is the case with human reason which, without the heavenly revelation, loses its purity and strength. When, therefore, a long period of time elapses without witnessing the appearance of any inspired one of God, it is but natural that reason, like earthly water, should become noxious and impure.

As an illustration of this principle, we may cast a glance at the pre-Islamic period. Before Prophet Muḥammad had appeared, darkness prevailed everywhere. About six hundred years had passed since the advent of Jesus Christ, and during this long interval no inspired one of God had made his appearance. The whole world witnessed to a falling off from purity and virtue, and corrupt ideas prevailed widely. This was due to no other factor but to the discontinuance of revelation. Reason, and not revelation, held sway and, on account of its imperfection and corruption, led people astray. The earthly water of human reason dried up because the heavenly water of inspiration had not come down upon earth for such a long time.

The Almighty directs the attention of men to His law that the earth's bringing forth of vegetation and verdure depends upon heavenly rain. This manifest law points to the secret law relating to revelation. Reason alone cannot be trusted, for its own existence is liable to decay if revelation does not afford it nourishment. When an inspired one of God appears upon the earth, his benevolence extends to all, and human reason is brightened and sharpened to a marked degree. There is a general search for truth and an animation and activity of all the dormant faculties is noticeable.

Such development of reason and zeal of the heart are the result of the blessed appearance of one who is a recipient of revelation. When you see, therefore, that there is a general quest for truth and that every one has begun to feel the need of faith, know it for certain that heavenly water has been poured down upon the earth.

SOURCES OF DIVINE KNOWLEDGE

"He is Allāh besides Whom there is no God :
The Knower of the unseen and the seen ; He
is the Beneficent, the Merciful" — 59 : 22.

Knowledge of certainty

As already stated, the Quran has described
three stages of knowledge: *'ilm al-yaqīn*, *'ain al-
yaqīn* and *ḥaq al-yaqīn*. Of these, *'ilm al-yaqīn* is
knowledge of a thing acquired inferentially as we
conclude the existence of fire from the presence
of smoke in a place without witnessing the fire.
But if we see the fire itself, our knowledge of the
existence of fire becomes a certainty of the second
degree — *'ain al-yaqīn*. Knowledge of a thing we
witness with the eye may, however, be further
improved upon through actual experience, for
instance, by thrusting our hand into the fire.
Thus we reach the highest stage of certainty,
which is *ḥaq al-yaqīn*.

The sources which guide us to the knowledge of certainty are reason and information. With reference to those who do not believe in these means, the Holy Quran says:

$$لَا يُكَلِّفُ اللهُ نَفْسًا إِلَّا وُسْعَهَا$$

"Allāh does not imposes on any soul a duty (which is) beyond its scope ... "[1] — 2 : 286.

$$وَقَالُوا لَوْ كُنَّا نَسْمَعُ أَوْ نَعْقِلُ مَا كُنَّا فِي أَصْحَابِ السَّعِيرِ ۝$$

"And they (disbelievers) say: Had we but listened or pondered, we should not have been among the inmates of the burning Fire"—67: 10.

The verses quoted above also point to the fact that a person can acquire the knowledge of certainty through accurate information. For instance, we have not seen London, nevertheless we are certain of the existence of a city of this name because we cannot disbelieve all those who have seen it. Or, though we did not see Aurangzeb yet it is beyond the shadow of doubt that he was one of the emperors who reigned in India.

Thus we can arrive at a certain conclusion as to the reality of a fact or the existence of a thing

---

1. In this verse, God gives us clearly to understand that the doctrines and beliefs to which He invites people through His messengers are only such as are within the capacity of human understanding and knowledge, and that He does not force men to bear any burden beyond their strength.

through hearing when the chain of testimony is strong. The inspiration of the prophets is a source of knowledge provided there has been no interruption in its transmission, and the vehicle through which it is conveyed to us is not of an imperfect nature. But if there are many different accounts of a single event contradicting each other, and they all claim to be based on revelation, the mere acceptance by any sect of some of these documents as of a heavenly origin, and the condemnation of the rest as spurious and fabricated, if not based on a critical inquiry, lends no support to the truth of the facts therein related. A series of such narratives, inconsistent with each other, is utterly incredible and we need no other proof for their rejection. Nor can they be a source of knowledge because they cannot lead to any certain conclusion, being themselves doubtful.

In this connection, it should be noted that the truth of the Quran does not depend merely on its uninterrupted transmission and authenticity, for it proceeds on the basis of reason. It does not compel us to accept its doctrines, principles and commandments simply on the authority of revelation, but appeals to our reason and supplies arguments in support of what it inculcates. It is to this fact that the Holy Book refers when it says that the principles which it inculcates are impressed in the nature of man :

$$وَهٰذَا ذِكْرٌ مُّبَارَكٌ$$

"And this is a blessed Reminder "[1] — 21 : 50.

$$لَا اِكْرَاهَ فِى الدِّيْنِ$$

"There is no compulsion in religion "[2] — 2:256.

$$وَشِفَآءٌ لِّمَا فِى الصُّدُوْرِهٖ$$

"And (it is) a healing for that which is in the breasts (a guidance) ... "[3] — 10 : 57.

The Quran is not a book which derives all its force from being an ancient document, which has been handed down to us through a safe course of transmission, but its real force lies in the sound arguments which it produces and the clear light which it sheds. In the same manner, intellectual arguments which have a sound basis lead a man to a knowledge of certainty. To this, the

1. This blessed Book does not preach strange and novel doctrines, but it is a Reminder of that which is impressed in the nature of man and the laws of Nature.

2. To all that which is talked about the Prophet of Arabia offering Islam or the sword as alternatives to the pagan Arabs, this verse is a sufficient answer. Islam does not compel a person to accept its doctrines, but offers reasons for their acceptance.

3. This verse means that the Quran is a cure for all spiritual ailments.

Word of God alludes in the following verses:

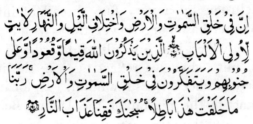

"In the creation of the heavens and the
earth and the alternation of the night and
the day, there are surely signs for men of
understanding. Those who remember Allāh
standing and sitting and (lying) on their sides,
and reflect on the creation of the heavens and
the earth: Our Lord, Thou hast not created
this in vain! Glory be to Thee! Save us from
the chastisement of the Fire" — 3 : 189-190.

Conscience, which is called human nature, is
also a source of knowledge. The Holy Book says:

فِطْرَتَ اللّٰهِ الَّتِیْ فَطَرَ النَّاسَ عَلَيْهَا

"The nature made by Allāh, in which
He has created men . . ." — 30 : 30.

This impression in the nature of man makes
him regard the Almighty as one without any
partner, the Creator of everything, and free from
subjection to birth or death. Although the
knowledge derived from human nature does not
appear to be inferential, yet we have called human

nature a source of knowledge because it leads to a conclusion by a very fine thread of inference. The Master has charged everything with a peculiar property which it is difficult to describe in definite words, but, when we reflect over it, the inherent property at once strikes the mind. If, for instance, we imagine the person of the Divine Being and ponder over the attributes we desire to see in Him and consider whether He should undergo the processes of birth and death and suffering like ourselves, the idea makes us shudder; human nature revolts at it and recoils from it, being unable to bear it. The idea is repellent. The still small voice within us at once speaks out that He, in Whose powers we must completely trust, should be a Perfect Being, free from every blemish and defect. The concepts of God and of the Unity of God co-exist in human nature, and the one is not separable from the other.

Knowledge through perception

But we could attain to a higher degree of certainty than that described above through *'ain al-yaqīn,* which means a direct knowledge of a thing as, for instance, in the material world we obtain the knowledge of a perfume through the sense of smell, that of the taste of edibles through the tongue and that of tangibility through the organs of touch.

All these experiences fall under the heading of *ain al-yaqīn*. But with respect to the life to come our knowledge attains this degree when we are directly inspired by God, hear His kind voice and experience His true revelations. Moreover, we feel this desire — the thirst for inspiration — in our hearts which is inexplicable unless we admit that the Merciful has provided the means of its satisfaction. Can we, in the present life which is the only gauge of the next and a nursery of it, remain contented with a blind faith based on tales and legends regarding the existence of the true, perfect, all-powerful and living Master, or be satisfied with the little effort of reason which has hitherto given to the world only imperfect and deficient knowledge of the Divine Being? Do not the lovers of God really desire that they should enjoy the bliss of speaking to their Creator? Can they, who have sacrificed everything for His sake and forsaken all their worldly interests, and who give their hearts and souls for Him, be content to stand in a dim light never to see the brilliant face of that shining sun of righteousness? Is it not true that the sweet Divine words "I am" furnish a better knowledge of His existence than all the reasoning of the philosophers, so much so that all their literature, seeking to prove the existence of God by the insufficient light of reason, is as nothing compared with these words?

In short, if the Beneficent has willed to give a
perfect knowledge of His own Self to the seekers-
after-truth, He has not shut the doors through
which they may be illumined by His word. In
this connection, the Quran teaches us this prayer:

اِهْدِنَا الصِّرَاطَ الْمُسْتَقِيمَ ۞ صِرَاطَ
الَّذِينَ اَنْعَمْتَ عَلَيْهِمْ ۖ

"Guide us on the right path, the path of those
upon whom Thou hast bestowed favours"—1:6-7.

It may be noted that "favours" here signify
the "heavenly blessings" which a person receives
directly from God, such as inspiration and revelation. In another verse we read:

لَهُمُ الْبُشْرَىٰ فِي الْحَيَوٰةِ الدُّنْيَا وَفِي الْاٰخِرَةِ

"For them (believers) is good news in this world's
life and in the Hereafter..." — 10:64.

Yet in another place, the Supreme Being says
the following with regard to the righteous people:

اِنَّ الَّذِينَ قَالُوا رَبُّنَا اللّٰهُ ثُمَّ اسْتَقَامُوا تَتَنَزَّلُ
عَلَيْهِمُ الْمَلَـٰٓئِكَةُ اَلَّا تَخَافُوا وَلَا تَحْزَنُوا وَ
اَبْشِرُوا بِالْجَنَّةِ الَّتِي كُنْتُمْ تُوعَدُونَ ۞

"Those who say, Our Lord is Allāh, then
continue in the right way, the angels descend

> upon them, saying: Fear not, nor be grieved,
> and receive good tidings of the Garden
> which you were promised " — 41 : 30.

This verse indicates that the righteous are
inspired by God in times of fear and grief, and
that angels are sent down for their consolation.

Meaning of inspiration

Before proceeding further, it seems necessary
to remove here a misconception regarding *ilham*
(inspiration). This word does not mean that an
idea is infused into the mind of a person who sets
himself to think about a thing. A poet is not
inspired in the theological sense when brilliant
ideas flash upon him as he sits down to write
poetry. In such a case, there is no distinction
between good and bad. When the mental powers
are applied to a subject, new ideas do flash
upon the mind according to the genius of the
thinker without any regard to the good or bad
nature of the subject.

If *ilhām* (inspiration) is taken to mean the
occurring of new ideas, a thief or dacoit or murderer
may as well be called *mulhām* (inspired one of God)
by virtue of the ingenious plans which may come
out of his evil mind for the perpetration of evil
deeds. Such a view of inspiration is held by those
who are ignorant of the Merciful Who bestows
peace and consolation upon the hearts of the

righteous and gives knowledge of spiritual truth to those who are not aware of them.

What is inspiration then? It is the living and powerful word of God in which He speaks to or addresses His servants whom He chooses from among the people. When these communications run on continually in a regular way — not being insufficient or fragmentary or enveloped in the darkness of evil ideas — and have a heavenly bliss, wisdom and power, they are the words of God with which He comforts His servants and reveals Himself to them. It is true that words are sometimes spoken to a man by way of trial but they are not accompanied with the perfection and blessings necessary to a true inspiration. In this early stage, a person is tried and he either stumbles on account of the weakness of the flesh or, having tasted of the sweet and life-giving fountain of inspiration, transforms himself and makes himself like those who have truly been inspired. If he does not walk in righteousness like the faithful servants, he is deprived of the favour and has nothing but vanity in his heart.

It should, moreover, be remembered that all those who receive inspiration are not of equal rank in the sight of God. Even the prophets, whose inspiration or revelation stands far above that of other men on account of its clearness, force and excellence, are not all on the same level. The Almighty says in the Quran:

تِلْكَ الرُّسُلُ فَضَّلْنَا بَعْضَهُمْ عَلَى بَعْضٍ

"We have (indeed) made some of these messengers to excel others ... " — 2 : 253.

From this, it appears that inspiration is but the Divine grace and does not interfere with the exaltation of degrees, for the latter depends upon the sincerity, devotion and faithfulness of a person towards the Supreme Being. Inspiration is also a fruit of these qualities. If an answer is vouchsafed when a person entreats his Lord, and there is no break or irregularity in the answers, and the word is accompanied with Divine majesty and light, and reveals the deep secrets of the future and hidden truths, there is no doubt that it is inspiration. It is necessary that between the Almighty and the recipient of such an inspiration there should be a close connection, such as exists in conversation between two intimate friends. When this person addresses his prayers, an answer is vouchsafed to him in sweet and eloquent words proceeding from the Creator, which is not the result of his own desires or of any deliberation or reflection on his part. Should he be continually graced with such words and answers, then surely the word which comes to him is the Divine word.

But this gift of pure and living words, revealed with clearness, and not mixed with low desires, is not granted to any but those whose hearts are filled with a high degree of faith and sincerity. True and pure inspiration reveals the mighty wonders of God. Very often, an effulgent light is created and with it comes a bright and majestic inspiration. What greater blessing or happiness can be conceived than speaking to the mighty Creator of the earth and heavens and being spoken to by Him?

It should, however, be noted that the mere utterance of words and phrases not distinctly recognized as having come from the Lord does not fall under the heading of inspiration. A person who finds himself in this condition is really being tried. For, the Almighty sometimes tries men who are remiss and negligent in the performance of their duties towards Him, by infusing certain words into their minds or causing them to be uttered, with respect to which they are like blind men not knowing whether the words come from God or Satan. A person who is thus tried should repent and reform himself.

The righteous man — to whom the doors of inspiration are open and who is spoken to by God in words which possess light, sweetness, majesty, deep significance and more than mortal wisdom, whose entreaties and supplications are answered

by Him as often as they are urged, who addresses
his supplications to Him repeatedly, and receives
answers thereto, whose prayers are accepted many
a time, who is informed of actual truths, excellent
points and deep secrets through inspiration —
must be thankful to the Lord and devote himself
entirely to Him. For, that person He chooses
out of His grace and mercy, and makes him an
heir to all the blessings which He has granted to
the righteous before. But it should be pointed
out that such a high Divine favour is seldom
bestowed, and to very few, and those to whom it
is granted consider every other blessing as naught
in comparison with this.

It may not be out of place to state here that it
is among the Muslims that individuals have always
been raised to this spiritual eminence. Islam is
the religion in which God draws His servants to
Him and speaks to them and through them. He
grants them all the blessings which He has ever
bestowed upon the righteous before. Ah! the
world is blind and does not know what a man
may attain to if he comes nearer to the Merciful.[1]

---

1.   It may be pointed out that people of the world do not care to take a
single step to attain nearness of God; but he who is a pilgrim on this path
is either declared heretic or is worshipped.   Both classes are guilty of
an iniquity: the one of excessive hatred and the other of excessive love.
But the wise man should adopt the mean course, neither reject him
whom the Lord Has chosen for this eminence nor bow down before him
whom He has created.

I would be guilty of an injustice if I were to conceal the fact that I have been raised to this spiritual eminence. The Almighty has favoured me with His word, and chosen me that I may give sight to the blind, lead the seekers-after-truth to the object of their search and give to the acceptors of truth the glad tidings of the pure fountain which is talked of by many, but is found by few. I can unhesitatingly say that, except by following the Quran, no one can find the true Lord in Whom lies the salvation of man and eternal bliss. It is my heart's inmost desire that others may see what I have seen and hear what I have heard; that they may forsake vain stories and run to accept the truth. That perfect source of knowledge which bring one to the noble presence of God, that pure heavenly water which washes off all doubts, that bright mirror through which the glory of the Master is revealed, is the word of God — the Divine inspiration.

I am certain that if the soul desires it earnestly, and the heart yearns for it, people should seek this way and set out in search of this path. But, how can this path be opened and the veil of ignorance removed? I assure all seekers-after-truth that it is Islam alone which promises this happy goal to the wayfarer and gives the glad tidings of this path of salvation. The true way to inspiration is open only to the followers of Prophet Muhammad.

Some people are of the opinion that the Lord has barred entrance to this way; such views are simply the invention of those who are themselves deprived of this heavenly blessing. Know it for certain, then, that as a person cannot hear without ears, cannot speak without tongue, and cannot see without eyes, in the same manner he cannot see the Beloved One without the Quran. The Almighty Whose grace is bounteous has never willed that He should close the door to inspiration and thus destroy the world. The gates are still wide open through which one can find entrance to the heavenly blessings of inspiration. But to seek it, a person must walk on the proper path and then only will he find it. That water of life came down from heaven and accumulated in a grand receptacle. To drink of it, he must reach it, stumbling and falling, and apply his lips to the cool and refrigerant water of life. In this consists the felicity of man that he should run to the spot where any trace is to be found of the Friend Whom he seeks. As light comes from heaven and sheds its lustre upon earth, the true light of guidance also comes from heaven.

It is not through talk or conjecture that a man can attain to the source of Divine knowledge. Are eyes of any avail in total darkness? If they are, then reason alone may be a guide to a perfect knowledge of God. The true Lord is not one

Whose lips are sealed and Who is, therefore, obliged to leave us to our own conjectures concerning Him. Nay, the perfect and living Creator has ever been giving unmistakable signs of His existence and He has even now willed to vouchsafe such signs to the present generation. The time is come when the doors of heaven shall be opened. Lo! the dawn is about to break forth. Blessed are they who rise up and seek the Almighty Whose lustre of glory never grows dim. The Quran says:

اللهُ نُورُ السَّمٰوٰتِ وَالْأَرْضِ

"Allāh is (indeed) the light of the heavens and the earth . . . " — 24 : 35.

It is from God that all light proceeds. He is the Sun of the sun, and the Life of all life, the True and Living Lord. Blessed is he who accepts Him!

Knowledge through sufferings

The other source of knowledge is that which is perfect in the highest degree and makes a man realize the certainty of the existence of God. This consists of the adversities and hardships which the prophets and the righteous are made to suffer at the hands of their enemies or by a heavenly decree. Sufferings make a man realize the full force of the legal injunctions which are thus illustrated in his practical life. Religious dogmas are mere theories and their perfection can be tested only through practice. A person who undergoes sufferings has an occasion to apply the treasure of knowledge accumulated in his heart to the actual circumstances of life, and by their right application he becomes, as it were, a perfect embodiment of Divine guidance.

The moral qualities, of whose knowledge the brain and the heart are the sole repositories at first, are displayed through actual practice in all the external and internal faculties; and forgiveness, revenge, patience, mercy, etc., are not mere names to such a person, but become realities which he has felt and seen, which thus make an impression upon his external and internal nature. On this point, the Supreme Being says:

وَلَنَبْلُوَنَّكُمْ بِشَيْءٍ مِّنَ الْخَوْفِ وَالْجُوعِ وَنَقْصٍ مِّنَ الْأَمْوَالِ
وَالْأَنْفُسِ وَالثَّمَرَاتِ ۗ وَبَشِّرِ الصَّابِرِينَ ۝ الَّذِينَ إِذَا أَصَابَتْهُمْ
مُّصِيبَةٌ ۙ قَالُوا إِنَّا لِلَّهِ وَإِنَّا إِلَيْهِ رَاجِعُونَ ۝ أُولَٰئِكَ عَلَيْهِمْ
صَلَوَاتٌ مِّن رَّبِّهِمْ وَرَحْمَةٌ ۖ وَأُولَٰئِكَ هُمُ الْمُهْتَدُونَ ۝

"And We shall certainly try you with something of fear and hunger and loss of property and lives and fruits. And give good news to the patient, who, when a misfortune befalls them say : 'Surely we are Allāh's, and to Him we shall

return.' Those are they on whom are blessings and mercy from their Lord; and those are
the followers of the right course"—2 : 155-157.

Here we are told that there is no great
excellence in mere knowledge which is treasured
in the heart or brain, but that the knowledge to be
valued is that which, on account of its application
to the practical course of life, gives a colouring to
a man's life. To improve and strengthen one's
knowledge, the best means is its application in
practice so that its impression is left not only upon
the mind but upon every faculty and limb.   In fact,
every sort of knowledge, however low its comparative value, is defective so long as it is untested
by practice.   It is to this that the Lord calls our
attention in the above verses. We are told that
our morals are not finally developed unless they
are proved by sufferings and trials which stand
to them in the relation of practice to knowledge:

لَتُبْلَوُنَّ فِىٓ أَمْوَالِكُمْ وَأَنْفُسِكُمْ وَلَتَسْمَعُنَّ مِنَ الَّذِينَ أُوتُوا
الْكِتَٰبَ مِن قَبْلِكُمْ وَمِنَ الَّذِينَ أَشْرَكُوٓا أَذًى كَثِيرًا وَ
إِن تَصْبِرُوا وَتَتَّقُوا فَإِنَّ ذَٰلِكَ مِنْ عَزْمِ الْأُمُورِ ۝

"You will certainly be tried in your property and
your persons. And you will certainly hear from
those who have been given the Book before you

and from the idolaters much abuse. And if
you are patient and keep your duty, surely
this is an affair of great resolution" — 3 : 185.

These verses show conclusively that knowledge
is not perfect and fruitful without practical application. Knowledge which is at its best in practice
is a source of blessings, but that which never passes
into the domain of the practical has no value.

Perfection in practice

The application of knowledge in practice is
what makes a man attain the highest stage of
certainty, for the truth of the certainty of a thing
cannot be realized unless every side of it is put
to a practical test. This is what happened in
Islam. Whatever injunctions are contained in
the Quran were beautifully illustrated in practice
in the life of Prophet Muḥammad and in the
lives of his companions who were thus enlightened
with true light. For the fulfilment of this purpose,
the All-Knowing divided the life of our Prophet
into two distinct periods: the period of sufferings,
adversities and persecutions, and the period of
triumph and prosperity. This was done in order
to provide occasion for the display of both sorts of
moral qualities: those which can be proved in time
of suffering, and those which cannot be proved
except in triumph and prosperity. In this way,
he had all his moral qualities brought to the test of

practice, and the two periods of his life enabled him to display them in the highest degree.

The thirteen years at Mecca represent the time of suffering, and a study of the life of Prophet Muhammad during that time shows clearly that there is not a single moral quality which could be manifested in suffering by the righteous that was not displayed by him. His complete trust in God, his refraining from showing the slightest impatience, his calm and serenity, his noble and dignified manner, his unshaken activity and zeal in the performance of the duties entrusted to him, his perseverance, his fearless courage, and numerous other moral qualities, so deeply impressed that even the unbelievers bore testimony to the great miracle of his perseverance under the hardest trials and sufferings and were ultimately convinced that all this was because of his perfect trust in the Supreme Being.

Then followed his life at Medina — a period of triumph, victory and prosperity, suited for the display of another division of moral qualities. His forgiveness, charity, sympathy, courage and other high moral qualities were so well displayed that a large number of the unbelievers embraced Islam. He freely forgave those who had persecuted and tortured him, extended shelter to those who had expelled him from Mecca, helped the poor among them, and showed kindness to his bitterest foes

when their lives were completely at his mercy.
The high morals thus displayed by Muḥammad
convinced the Arabs that their Prophet could
not but be from God, and a truly righteous
man. Their invertebrate hatred was by these
noble morals at once converted into fast friendship.

One of these great and noble moral qualities
is described in the following verse:

قُلْ اِنَّ صَلَاتِى وَنُسُكِى وَمَحْيَاىَ وَمَمَاتِى لِلّٰهِ رَبِّ الْعٰلَمِيْنَ ۞

"Say: My prayer and my sacrifice and
my life and my death are surely for
Allāh, the Lord of the worlds " — 6 : 163.

It should not be imagined that death in the
way of God and for the good of mankind, here
spoken of, means that the Prophet was under any
delusion like ignorant and insane people that a
suicidal end of his own life would, in any way,
benefit others. Nay, he hated all such ideas and
the Quran regarded those who entertain these
notions as guilty of a serious crime:

وَلَا تُلْقُوْا بِاَيْدِيْكُمْ اِلَى التَّهْلُكَةِ ۛ وَاَحْسِنُوْا

"And cast not yourselves to perdition with your
own hands and do good (to others)" — 2:195.

It is a plain truth that one man cannot relieve
another of headache by breaking his own head.

Such a step is at the best an unwise act. In short,
the reference to the Prophet's death in the way
of God and for the benefit of mankind simply
denotes that Muḥammad had devoted his life to
the service and welfare of mankind out of sympathy,
and that with his prayers and preaching, and the
adoption of every wise method for the regeneration
of his people, as well as by bearing patiently their
persecutions, he sacrificed his own life and all his
comforts in this path. With reference to this
sacrifice of his life, the Quran elsewhere says:

$$لَعَلَّكَ بَاخِعٌ نَّفْسَكَ أَلَّا يَكُونُوا مُؤْمِنِينَ ۝$$

"Perhaps thou (Muḥammad) wilt kill thyself
with grief because they believe not" — 26 : 3.

$$فَلَا تَذْهَبْ نَفْسُكَ عَلَيْهِمْ حَسَرَاتٍ ۚ$$

"So let not thy soul waste away in grief for them
(Allāh is Knower of what they do) " — 35 : 8.

The way in which a man may sacrifice his life
for his people is to encounter all difficulties, and
work hard for their welfare by adopting measures
which are likely to better their condition.

It is mere folly to think that true sacrifices for a
people, who are deeply immersed in sin or involved in error, consist in committing suicide. To

regard this act of folly as leading to the salvation of those who have gone astray is the height of absurdity. It betrays, if not want of sense, at least a weakness of character and a lack of moral courage. It is a faint-hearted man who seeks shelter in death from the difficulties which he is unable to face. In whatever way may suicide be explained afterwards, it cannot be doubted that it is an act of folly resulting from weakness of mind.

In order to furnish a perfect example of high moral qualities, a man must pass through prosperity as well as adversity. If he is persecuted and subjected to sufferings and hardships, and has no occasion of wreaking his vengeance on his enemies, he cannot be said to possess the quality of forgiveness of injuries. What he would have done if he had the power to avenge himself on his enemies is impossible to ascertain. To know that a man possessed high moral qualities it is, therefore, not sufficient to know that he showed meekness and forbearance when he was powerless against his enemies and was persecuted by them, but also that he freely forgave those enemies when he was completely triumphant, and when they were completely at his mercy.

If he never went into the field of battle, his courage would be a moot point, and we could not say whether he would have shown martial daring or cowardice. If he never experienced affluence, it would be difficult to say whether he would have amassed riches or given them in charity. The grace of God granted the Prophet suitable opportunities for the display of all kinds of morals such as meekness, charity, courage, forgiveness, justice, etc., in a highly excellent degree which is without a parallel in history.[1]

It may be added here that it is a fact that forgiveness was not extended to the implacable foes of Islam who were bent upon the extirpation of Truth, and who ruthlessly massacred the innocent Muslims or put them to excruciating tortures and cruel persecutions. Pardon to such people would have meant the annihilation of the righteous believers.

---

1. The error of the opponents of Islam lies in a misconception of the attributes of the Divine Being. They think that a revealed law should, on no account and under no circumstances whatsoever, enjoin a resistance of evil or the punishment of evil-doers, and that Divine love and mercy should not be manifested except in the form of meekness. With them the most reverential attitude towards God consists in limiting His perfect attributes to humbleness and lowliness. This is a serious error. Anyone who can think for himself will see that the Divine laws of Nature, though they are a mercy for mankind, are not always manifested in a mild and gentle form. The Divine Physician out of His infinite mercy, gives us sometimes sweet syrup to drink and, out of His mercy too, administers a bitter dose on other occasions. Both are manifestations of His mercy. Thus it is His mercy which requires that the wicked should be destroyed when He sees that they aim at the extirpation of the righteous and act corruptly on the earth and shed innocent blood. For this purpose, He sends punishment upon the wicked either from earth or from heaven, for He is as Wise as He is Merciful.

The object of the wars undertaken by the Muslims at the bidding of Prophet Muḥammad was not to cause bloodshed. They had been expelled from their homes to seek shelter elsewhere and many innocent Muslims, men and women, had been murdered in cold blood. But their relentless persecutors had not stopped there. In obedience to the Divine commandment of self-defence, the sword was allowed to be taken up against those who had drawn the sword for the utter extirpation of Islam:

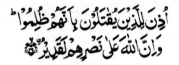

"Permission (to fight) is given to those on whom war is made, because they are oppressed. And surely Allāh is able to assist them"[1] — 22 : 39.

The object of these wars was, therefore, to remedy an evil by abating the bloodshed caused by the persecutors of the believers. Had the

---

1. According to authentic reports, this is the earliest permission given to Muslims to fight. There is nothing to show that this verse was not revealed at Mecca. On the other hand, it was owing to this revelation that in the well-known oath of allegiance taken at Aqaba, Prophet Muḥammad required a promise from the Medina deputation that they would defend him against his enemies just as they would defend their own children. The words in which the permission is granted show clearly that war was first made on the Muslims by their opponents; and secondly, that the Muslims had already suffered great oppressions at the hands of their persecutors — Publisher.

faithful Muslims not defended themselves under these circumstances against the outrages of their cruel persecutors, the result would have been the slaughter of more innocent lives, including women and children, and Islam would have been nipped in the bud.

Books on Islam

Ahmadiyya Anjuman Isha'at Islam, Lahore, U.S.A.

" *Probably no man living has done longer or more valuable service for the cause of Islamic revival than Maulana Muhammad Ali of Lahore. His literary works, with those of the late Khwaja Kamal-ud-Din, have given fame and distinction to the Ahmadiyya Movement*" –
M. Pickthall, famous British Muslim and translator of Holy Quran.

Books by Maulana Muhammad Ali:

The Holy Qur'an   ISBN: 0-913321-01-X   Pp. lxxvi + 1256

Arabic text, with English translation, exhaustive commentary, comprehensive Introduction, and large Index. Leading English translation. Has since 1917 influenced millions of people all over the world. Model for all later translations. Thoroughly revised in 1951.

"To deny the excellence of Muhammad Ali's translation, the influence it has exercised, and its proselytising utility, would be to deny the light of the sun" – Maulana Abdul Majid Daryabadi, leader of orthodox Muslim opinion in India.

"The first work published by any Muslim with the thoroughness worthy of Quranic scholarship and achieving the standards of modern publications" – Amir Ali in The Student's Quran, London, 1961.

The Religion of Islam ISBN: 0-913321-32-X *1983 retypeset edition*, Pp. 647

Comprehensive and monumental work on the sources, principles, and practices of Islam. First published 1936.

"...an extremely useful work, almost indispensable to the students of Islam" – Dr Sir Muhammad Iqbal, renowned Muslim philosopher.

"Such a book is greatly needed when in many Muslim countries we see persons eager for the revival of Islam, making mistakes through lack of just this knowledge" – 'Islamic Culture', October 1936.

A Manual of Hadith   ISBN: 0-913321-15-X   Pp. 400

Sayings of Holy Prophet Muhammad on practical life of a Muslim, classified by subject. Arabic text, English translation and explanatory notes.

Muhammad The Prophet ISBN: 0-913321-07-9 *1984 retypeset edition*, Pp. 208

Researched biography of Holy Prophet, sifting authentic details from spurious reports. Corrects many misconceptions regarding Holy Phophet's life.

Early Caliphate ISBN: 0-913321-27-3   *1983 retypeset edition*, Pp. 214

History of Islam under first four Caliphs.

"(1) Muhammad The Prophet, (2) The Early Caliphate, by Muhammad Ali together constitute the most complete and satisfactory history of the early Muslims hitherto compiled in English" – 'Islamic Culture', April 1935.

Living Thoughts of Prophet Muhammad ISBN: 0-913321-19-2   Pp. 150

Life of Holy Prophet, and his teachings on various subjects.

The New World Order   ISBN: 0-913321-33-8   Pp. 170

Islam's solution to major modern world problems.

Founder of the Ahmadiyya Movement   ISBN: 0-913321-61-8   Pp. 100

Biography of Hazrat Mirza by Maulana Muhammad Ali who worked closely with him for the last eight years of the Founder's life.

Bayan-ul-Quran   ISBN: 0-913321-21-4   Pp. 1539

Encyclopedic Urdu translation and commentary of the Holy Qur'an

Muhammad in World Scriptures by Maulana Abdul Haque Vidyarthi (in 3 Vols.)   ISBN: 0-913321-59-1

Prophecies about the Holy Prophet Muhammad in all major world scriptures

Ahmadiyyat in the Service of Islam, by Naseer A. Faruqui.   Pp. 149
         ISBN: 0-913321-00-1

The Teachings of Islam by Hazrat Mirza Ghulam Ahmad.   Pp. 226

Brilliant, much-acclaimed exposition of the Islamic path for the physical, moral and spiritual progress of man, first given as a lecture in 1896.   ISBN: 0-913321-34-6

Muhammad and Christ by Maulana Muhammad Ali   Pp. 97
         ISBN: 0-913321-19-2

Antichrist Gog and Magog by Maulana Muhammad Ali   Pp. 72
         ISBN: 0-913321-04-4

Introduction to the Study of the Holy Quran   Pp. 133
by Maulana Muhammad Ali   ISBN: 0-913321-06-0

Introduction to Islam by Zahid Aziz, M. Sc. Phd., *"Editor of the Light and Islamic Review"*   ISBN: 0-913321-08-7   Pp. 66

Over 100 basic questions answered for beginners and younger readers.

Testimony of the Holy Quran by Hazrat Mirza Ghulam Ahmad

A discussion by *Hazrat Mirza Ghulam Ahmad* on his claim of being the *Promised Messiah* based on the *Holy Quran*.   ISBN: 0-913321-43-5   Pp. 103

Sources of Christianity by Khwaja Kamal-ud-Din, Founder of the *Woking Mission* and the journal *The Islamic Review*.   Pp. 108

This book shows how the Doctrine of Trinity, sonship of God and the Atonement of sins have pagan origins.   ISBN: 0-913321-58-3

Islam My Only Choice by Khwaja Kamal-ud-Din, Founder of the *Woking Mission* and the journal *The Islamic Review*.   ISBN: 0-913321-54-0   Pp. 37

The Ideal Prophet by Khwaja Kamal-ud-Din, Founder of the *Woking Mission* and the journal *The Islamic Review*.   ISBN: 0-913321-53-2   Pp. 191

Alhamdolillah (Praise be to Allah) by Fazeel Sahukhan. This Children's board Book introduces Islamic phrases in an attractively Illustrated story form.   ISBN: 0-913321-51-6   Pp. 20

For prices and delivery of these books and inquiries about other books and free literature, please contact: **A.A.I.I.**

1315 Kingsgate Rd.,
Columbus, Ohio, 43221 U.S.A.
Phone (614) 457-8504
Fax   (614) 457-4455   PRINTED IN CANADA